Praise for *Rebuilding Broken Systems*

"Miszewski's book is a powerful call to action for the next generation of leaders. He provides a practical road map for young professionals in public service, showing them exactly how to navigate and fix the broken systems they are inheriting. This is essential reading for anyone early in their career who wants their work in government to truly matter."

—Jim Doyle,
Former Governor, State of Wisconsin

"For young professionals in philanthropy, this book is a revelation. Miszewski clearly outlines how foundations must partner across all four forces— foundations, nonprofits, government, and corporations—to achieve sustainable change. *Rebuilding Broken Systems* is the playbook our emerging changemakers need to move beyond traditional grantmaking and truly empower communities."

—Angelique Power,
CEO of Skillman Foundation

"*Rebuilding Broken Systems* is an essential tool for every young professional in the nonprofit sector. Miszewski provides an invaluable map showing how our work in the nonprofit world is deeply connected to government, philanthropy, and the corporate world. This book will inspire and empower the next generation of nonprofit leaders to think bigger and demand systemic change."

—Walter J. Lanier,
CEO of Great Lakes Urban Empowerment

"Miszewski proves that the business of business is *more* than just business; it's about social impact. And more importantly, does your impact drive outcomes like we enable organizations to do at Impact Genome? This book is the definitive guide for early-career professionals who demand that their work aligns with their values. It provides a clear framework for how purpose-driven companies can collaborate with the other three forces to build a better, more just society."

—Jason Saul,
CEO of Mission Measurement

MATT MISZEWSKI

REBUILDING BROKEN SYSTEMS

Bringing Companies, Governments, Foundations, and Nonprofits Together to **Save Communities**

WILEY

For general information on our other products and services or for technical support, please contact our Customer Care Department within the United States at (800) 762-2974, outside the United States at (317) 572-3993 or fax (317) 572-4002.

Wiley also publishes its books in a variety of electronic formats. Some content that appears in print may not be available in electronic formats. For more information about Wiley products, visit our website at www.wiley.com.

Library of Congress Cataloging-in-Publication Data is Available:

ISBN: 9781394313150 (cloth)
ISBN: 9781394313167 (ePub)
ISBN: 9781394313174 (ePDF)

Cover Design: Jon Boylan
Cover Image: © ozzichka/stock.adobe.com
Author Photo: Courtesy of the Author
Printed and bound by CPI Group (UK) Ltd, Croydon, CR0 4YY

C9781394313150_120226

This book is dedicated to my incredible wife, Kathleen O'Toole. She has shown me that commitment to always doing what's right despite the odds or equity is the difference between living a good life and living well. She inspires me daily with her ability to shoulder her challenges and never shrug, deal with intransigent problems and never lose her smile, and work through an unfair world without letting it decrease the joy she brings to everyone around her. I am better because of her.

Contents

Introduction

By intention the title of this book, *Rebuilding Broken Systems*, is a challenge and an invitation. Perhaps you share my conviction that our democratic society is in a period of crisis. That's the challenge. My belief is that, regardless of how far up the ladder you have climbed, by doing the hard and at times uncomfortable work of rediscovering our common ground and rebuilding our institutions on that common ground, we can fix it. That's the invitation. And the reward.

The point of this book is to provide a guide especially addressing early-stage and mid-career professionals working in the four forces of civil society, namely nonprofits, philanthropy, governments, and corporates. Reading these chapters will provide a deeper understanding of the connectedness among the four forces and how redefining their roles and realigning their goals are the accelerants to achieving meaningful and sustainable social change.

Over the course of my career, I have worked for impact in all four forces. In the public sector I was proud to serve as counsel for most of the public sector unions in the country, I served as State Director of SEIU in Wisconsin and Senior Counsel for AFSCME DC48, Chief Information Officer for Wisconsin Governor Jim Doyle, and a US Congressional staffer for the incredible Congressman Jerry Kleczka who served on the Ways and Means Committee. My corporate experience included being GM for Microsoft's and SVP for Salesforce's Global Government businesses, then, as head of Global Sales and Marketing, helping to grow Digital Realty Trust's enterprise value from $8B to $42B. Next, I ran global revenue for open government leader Socrata, which was later acquired by Tyler Technologies and was the CEO of AkitaBox, a great SaaS startup in the building and architectural sectors.

My understanding of the nonprofit and philanthropic sectors carried throughout my entire career. From advising labor unions as a young lawyer to working with communities in the Doyle Administration to helping every corporation I was a part of give back to the community. But the culmination of this lifelong learning is the result of my recent years as CEO at Catchafire, Inc., whose work supports tens of thousands of nonprofits around the world through deals with major Foundations and Fortune 500 companies worldwide. In addition, my training as a civil rights lawyer helped me develop a systematic view of society and its complex challenges. It is service in each of the four forces directly that has given me the insights to help guide the next great shift in American society.

On a systems level, *Rebuilding Broken Systems* advocates for practical policy changes in each sector to help build a stable foundation upon which change can occur. But on a more personal level, *Rebuilding Broken Systems* is a call to action across all four forces and across generations to support this new breed of young professionals as they seek to find purpose in their careers by doing values-aligned work that matters.

Researching this book rewarded me with the opportunity to learn more about the extraordinary work being done by exceptional changemakers. Each chapter begins with a quote from one of these wise folks. Chapter 8 contains lightly edited transcripts of my longer conversations with each of them, included for the express purpose of inspiring and informing us about the ways people are making a difference today by tackling social needs that they hold especially urgent and important. Taken as a whole, this chapter provides a rich and inclusive view of the various people and perspectives bringing about change by reimagining and rebuilding their respective institutions and communities.

For those who feel hopeless or disengaged, I want this book to uncover a path forward that empowers and encourages them to push for significant and systemic changes wherever they may currently work. My hope is that readers will realize they are not alone in their aspirations or in their battles. With some attainable policy and process changes, their desire to create a better and more just society is within reach.

Rebuilding Broken Systems offers a much-needed realistic approach to building new institutions moored to a unique pairing of American justice and hope. Practical, comprehensive, and thought-provoking, *Rebuilding Broken Systems* serves as a timely, essential road map for all business leaders, social activists, philanthropists, and nonprofit professionals looking to bring about real change in the world.

Persevere!

PART 1

The Problem in the Four Forces

CHAPTER 1

The System Is Broken, but We Can Fix It

*"When you think about how financiers come in and fund
things, there's different types of financing for different
functions in an entity or a business or an advancing project.
And each one of these four, the corporate, the foundations,
the nonprofit, the government has a piece of a puzzle to play
to solve social ills and their money should come in
differently."*

**—Walter Lanier, President and CEO,
Great Lakes Urban Empowerment Solutions**

Hope or fear. Elation or despair. Confidence or anxiety. For many,
the outcome of the 2024 US election placed you squarely on
one side or the other of these extreme emotions. If there was one
theme throughout the endless campaigning it was divisiveness. The
polls, the pundits, and the loudest voices kept stressing how splin-
tered we had become as a nation. There was even talk about a possible civil war.

It's my belief that the serious fractures in democracy many are
just now recognizing have been quietly but dramatically developing
for decades. Since the 1980s we as a nation have drifted further
away from supporting the balanced infrastructure a stable democracy depends upon: the strong, collaborative, and coordinated

actions of philanthropy, nonprofits, government, and corporations. Despite the weakening or destruction of many institutions, these four types of institutions, working together and playing to their unique strengths, can meet all the needs of all citizens. That might sound overly hopeful, but my deeply held belief is based on decades of life in the trenches.

So why do so many of us, whether we're politically on the left or the right, feel that our country is heading in the wrong[1] direction and that America's best days are behind us? Although many of us are truly dedicated to building a brighter future and stronger communities, why do we perceive our systems as failing?

The answer is complicated and the solution not simple, but it is in times of crisis that we as a country have found the will to change and the momentum to reinvent our society (if you remember 9/11, you saw our best selves up close). Starting in this chapter, this book examines the ways in which we have increasingly abandoned our foundational institutions. It points out how our evolving demographics require a new, more pluralistic vision of governance. It argues for how we can rebuild the pillars of democracy without giving in to a revolution of mindless destruction. And finally, the book lays out a vision for reimagining how philanthropy, nonprofits, government, and corporations can reclaim their respective abilities to make America live up to her original promise by addressing our common needs and committing to solving our shared social, economic, and environmental challenges. As the Kondratieff wave theory[2] illustrates, societies evolve slowly, typically over eras lasting between 40 to 50 years. Transformation often occurs rapidly near the end of such periods of change, such as Japan underwent after WWII. In the United States, we find ourselves in the midst of a major era shift. Our time to shape that change is now.

OK, That's a Lot

Over the past several decades we have collectively drifted away from key beliefs held by previous generations. As support for strong central government and established religions, confidence in large corporations, and a sense of civic or charitable obligations have all eroded, it is increasingly less apparent where we place our trust for creating and maintaining an equitable, thriving society. If all of these institutions are failing us, where do we look for hope and leadership?

Two data points to consider. When Lyndon Johnson took office in 1964, during the Vietnam War by the way, 77% of American citizens expressed approval of and faith in the government. When Joe Biden became president in 2020, 20% of the population had faith in the government.[3] A nearly 60-point drop in just under 60 years has to give you pause.

Less dramatic but still significant is the decline in religious affiliation. While the majority of Americans profess a belief in God, attendance at religious services continues to decline.

Trust in corporations is perhaps more difficult to measure, though it has been shown to have economic value.[4] Consumer perception is one indicator, but employee loyalty and retention can be another. Certainly the era of a "job for life" is long gone, taking with it pensions and the promise of a financially secure retirement. Millennials and Gen Z workers have been told to expect multiple changes of employers and careers, and "job hopping" as opposed to "climbing the ladder" is seen as the best route to advancement. Overall, there is no longer a belief that corporations can exist to solve social problems. They exist to provide jobs. This is a big departure from where some of the corporations in our country started: steel, automotive, or other manufacturing businesses that invested heavily in building the communities where they did business. In the 1980s President Ronald Reagan lit the match when he convinced us that businesses exist solely for profit.[5] That gave corporations the green light to stop investing in their local cities and small towns. Bust the unions, send jobs offshore, move your headquarters for tax breaks. These behaviors erased our expectations that corporations will make contributions of any significant kind in support of community needs.

Because nonprofits rely on grants and donations to fund their work, donor fatigue is a serious threat to their[6] existence. The rise of social media and fundraising via text messages has enabled many more parties to reach more potential donors with requests to fund a vast array of urgent needs. How much of the mail that arrives in your mailbox at home is soliciting donations? How many of these do you even open let alone send money to? The demand seems to far exceed our giving ability.

Philanthropy, too, is barely recognizable compared to the early days of individual giving by the extremely wealthy, industrialist moguls of the late nineteenth and early twentieth century such as the Carnegies, Mellons, and Rockefellers. While concentration of wealth among the top 1% of US citizens has accelerated in the twenty-first century, the holistic sense of civic obligation felt by earlier philanthropists is far less evident. In addition, regulations have been imposed on all philanthropic organizations that curtail the impact the trillions of dollars under their management could have.

When we put all these pieces side by side, we have the general perception that there is no singular institution *both willing and able* to deliver the things we all want. The desires I will identify as our common ground; namely public safety, affordable health care, a good education for our children, rewarding employment, and the guarantee of retirement with dignity.

Admittedly this appears to paint a grim picture. Overlay the flames of divisiveness that have cynically been fanned, especially during the past 10 years. But my experience in these four sectors leads me to believe we are not beyond hope or redemption. Rediscovering our commonalities and having the courage to build what we fundamentally believe in, across all identities, can break the political fever gripping much of our society and holding us back from societal progress. Reconstructing these four forces— government, corporations, nonprofit, and philanthropy—in order to rebuild our social safety net is now paramount to our efforts to save this great nation. And the great news is that many of us do care deeply. We just need these four forces to learn to and commit to working together.

Who Is "We" in "We the People"?

The many granular analyses of the 2024 election made plain the demographic shifts underway in the United States.[7] A declining birth rate and an increase in residents that are people of color is not so subtly changing the face of America. Boomers aging out, women becoming more than 50% of the population, a growing wealth and income gap, a lack of affordable housing, and a perception of an economy that benefits the wealthy all contribute to the complexity of who we are and what matters to us.

We are seeing a realignment of population along party lines, with the working class and some minority groups fleeing the Democratic Party and signing on to Republican promises. The migration of Latino males and young Black men joining the historic ranks of older white male Republicans offers an excellent example of how a one-size fits-all politics must give way to a new pluralism.[8] It's the only way to meet the aspirations of such a mismatched assemblage of voters. Political parties on both sides have to recognize that multiple factions have equal rights to have their concerns addressed. The "New Majority" will arise from a focus on issues such as those already mentioned, namely public safety, affordable health care, education, rewarding employment, and retirement with dignity. These concerns align on interests, not identities. Such commonly held goals bridge the areas of impact each of the four forces can bring about if they work in tandem. Exploring what this could look like is the central concern of this book.

As the United States inevitably becomes more ethnically, culturally, and socially diverse, it is apparent that a new hybrid approach is needed not just for governing but for developing the sustainable resources required to promote a just and equitable society for us all.

A New Compact: Rebuild on Common Ground

Those who have lost hope in the American dream or who are discouraged by the enormity of issues we face may advocate for letting the system collapse. Let it devolve under the weight of poor leadership or give way to willfully destructive forces with their own agenda. In this book I'll explore another way, not the type of imperialism that only allows for clear winners and vanquished losers. We can envision an endgame that is not achieved through mindless destruction or apathetic surrender. Let's repurpose the very process used to form this country, revolution. A form of revolution that does not tear down but builds up from a strong and inclusive base. A future that clearly sees win-win solutions for us all. **Let's rebuild on common ground**. Of course that means compromise. Yes, it demands meeting in the middle. It only works when we create, recognize, and support new relationships and coalitions based on shared values.

We must forge a new compact among these four forces, an agreement demanded by all of us who believe a better world is attainable. It will take many of us leaning on these four powerful forces already existing in our world and requiring them to adapt. I contend and hope to demonstrate that we have everything we need to bring about this change if we move from a scarcity mindset and zero-sum game approach to one of collectively achieved, broadly experienced gain.

Filling the Institutional Vacuum

When we begin to feel we can no longer rely on organizations or leaders in times of need, democracy falters. We have seen this internationally when economies collapse, ethnic tensions burst out, and uncertainty and fear prompt people to turn to a played-out "strongman" solution. We have the opportunity to remake the four forces of our society, and these institutions have the chance to regain the public trust. As we'll discuss, convening the influencers and leaders of philanthropy, nonprofits, government, and corporations and helping them to find a collaborative way forward can restore the scaffolding our unique democracy depends upon.

Specifically, we will call on each of these four institutions to do what only they can do best, but from now on working not in disconnected silos but together in tight collaboration.

- ◆ Philanthropy can intervene at critical times to support social impact efforts over the short term by investing more of its vast financial resources now comprising trillions of dollars.
- ◆ Nonprofits supply the "feet on the street" and are best positioned to carry out the programs and initiatives promoting social well-being. They can operate effective food banks but struggle to "solve" the problem of hunger.
- ◆ Government is the single best provider of infrastructure, both physical (roads, bridges) and social (education, health services) requiring large investments of capital over long time horizons. But the system for tackling such projects and infrastructure itself must be built anew.

◆ Corporate has the ability to address structural social and economic issues because they have the necessary financial resources and stability to tackle big challenges. A change in mindset could divert some portion of profits out of CEO's compensation packages and into civic investment. This must be accompanied by a vocal belief in a new brand, restoring a stronger civic society and resulting in more durable foundations.

Until we can redefine and realign these four forces and in the process create a robust structural support we will remain in freefall, unable to affect the positive change we could collectively make happen. Citizens have proven that they care enough to engage during this most recent election for president when they cast the second-highest vote count in US history.[9] Now we have an obligation to provide our fellow Americans with a structure that unites them . . . on common ground.

Summary and What's Ahead

In this chapter we have started to deeply understand the challenges in modern society through the lens of the four forces: nonprofits, foundations, corporations, and government. We have gone through the history of the drift away from solid institutions and the challenges that a further drift toward distrust in institutions has brought us. We have also understood in depth who we are as Americans, how we can build a new social contract together, and how we can utilize the four forces to rebuild our institutions to capture community strength.

Chapters 2–5 will examine each of the four forces: philanthropy, nonprofits, government, and corporations in greater detail. Each chapter will provide some historical context for the origins and evolution, along with examples of notable failures and inspiring successes. In addition, there will be illuminating insights from current leaders in each of these entities.

The remainder of the book lays out what my experience, observation, interactions, readings, and reflection have led me to see as a way forward. Ultimately mine is a message of hope and encouragement for how to move forward with the ideas presented in this book. It's a call to action, especially aimed at early and mid-stage career professionals in business, government, nonprofits, and philanthropy. And for everyone else who wants to be the change they want to see.

And throughout the chapters ahead I will mention one particularly interesting enabler, Artificial Intelligence. This tool in its current form is inaccessible at scale for those fighting for stronger communities. But the latest additions to this burgeoning technology change that and I will talk briefly throughout the book about how you can leverage it for your work.

CHAPTER 2

Philanthropy in the Billions

"Good risk-taking by philanthropists can be enormously helpful developing the data and the experience for government to come along later . . . What you don't want to have happen is for private philanthropy to take over the government's responsibility. The government has a responsibility here, and the government can't back away and say, 'Let's have people do it.'"
—James Doyle, Former Governor of Wisconsin

Philanthropy is an enormous topic, intimidating to take on holistically. So, where should we begin in attempting to rebuild this space? A good place to start is with some big numbers and a working definition of philanthropy.

First, the numbers.

- ◆ $1.7 trillion. The amount of money philanthropic organizations and foundations currently hold in their endowments.[1]
- ◆ 813. The 2024 number of billionaires in the United States,[2] up from 66 billionaires in 1990.[3]
- ◆ 22 million. The number of millionaires in the United States (40% of global millionaires)[4] up from approximately 1.5 million in 1990.

◆ $5.4 trillion. The combined 2024 net worth of the 400 wealthiest people in America.[5]

◆ $557.16 billion. The amount given to charities by US individuals, organizations, and corporations in 2023.[6]

Next, a definition and some clarifications.

The word *philanthropy* has Greek roots, roughly translating into "man-loving," but in its more inclusive sense it refers to an altruistic application of private assets to create public good. Overall, the goal of philanthropy is to contribute to the general well-being of humanity by addressing root cause problems and financially supporting sustainable solutions.

While charity and philanthropy are sometimes used interchangeably, for our purposes this chapter focuses on philanthropy and its potential for broader, longer-term impact. Charity may take the form of individual giving for immediate results, like donating to winter coat drives or food banks. Philanthropy at scale with its far greater resources aims to address pressing social problems by investing in education, public health, homelessness, racial inequality, and solutions for other major issues confronting society. Its activities differ from corporate initiatives, which are *private* initiatives, and generally for material gain; and are unlike government programs, which are *public* initiatives for the common good demanding deep and sustained investment, such as providing general public services and infrastructure.

Next let's go back to the numbers and the story they tell.

Some of the highlights from Giving USA's[7] 2024 annual report[8] include:

◆ Roughly $374.40 billion in donations by individuals
◆ An estimated $103.53 billion by foundations
◆ More than $42 billion made through bequests in trusts and wills
◆ More than $36 billion in corporate donations

If you do the math, the dollars pile up impressively. There is undeniably a great deal of money and financial clout available to the philanthropic sector. It is clear that the existence of capital is not holding anyone back. So why do our social problems not only persist but seem to worsen over time?

In my view there are multiple factors blunting the impact philanthropy could have.

Undeniably we have seen a **cultural shift away from philanthropy despite a rapidly growing millionaire and billionaire class**. Unlike the twentieth-century Carnegie-level givers, those privileged folks in the exponentially expanding sphere of billionaires demonstrate no similar sense of civic obligation. And when they do give generously, they often do so with strings and obligations attached making the donations less impactful. And the general public, rather than expressing dismay at this stinginess, seems to marvel at the consumption excesses of the wealthy. We no longer expect them to "give back." An America that once lauded the engaged industrialist of the Gilded Age now celebrates a new angry and never-ending accumulation of wealth with little care for supporting the communities they came from.

Rapid growth in personal worth is not limited to the uber-rich. Across the United States we have witnessed the **stratification of significant wealth**.[9] The number of households with assets in excess of 1 million dollars continues to grow. Families with personal worth of more than 100 million, or 50–100 million, or 10–50 million, or even 1–10 million now have resources their families could only dream of. Although they cannot donate on the level of the uber-wealthy, they now have multiple routes for charitable giving enabling them to enjoy highly attractive **tax breaks** similar to those taken advantage of by the uber-rich. But, unlike the industrialists of past eras, there is no organized effort to train this new upper class in the obligations that come with the acquisition of wealth.

What once were well-intentioned **regulatory constraints** placed by the government on philanthropic organizations have become impediments to granters as well as grantees. For example, to ensure that the rich were not simply dodging taxes by contributing to philanthropic organizations, the government imposed a requirement that these institutions grant ~5% of their endowment annually. Over time what was intended to be a floor for giving has become in many instances a ceiling.

We see this unfortunate misperception played out in the mis-placed emphasis foundations put on the **preservation of capital**. The market shocks of the pandemic sent many foundations rushing to cut grants and eliminate established programs that nonprofits, and communities, depended on, claiming that their endowments had been severely depleted by the market downturn. However, when the market returned those funds were not necessarily replenished. The level of need in the community did not change. This set of actions protected the endowments that were created to be perpetual.

Finally, and very importantly, we are seeing the fallout from a **lack of sustained coordination** of effort among philanthropic organizations and the other three forces of society, namely *nonprofits, businesses, and government*. This book seeks to expose this lack of coordination and make the argument that our society's failure to remedy social problems is not from a lack of capital or resources. It is a pronounced failure of distribution of capital already in play.

I believe we must fix this.

Your Grandfather's Philanthropy

When practiced at scale, philanthropy is a powerful legacy builder. Who doesn't recognize the names of some of the most legendary twentieth-century US philanthropists, Carnegie, Rockefeller, and Ford? While you may have disdain for how they accumulated their vast fortunes or perhaps you disagree with their politics, the extent of their giving is indisputable. These hugely successful businessmen believed that their extraordinary financial success brought with it an obligation to invest significantly in their communities and in the public good. As Andrew Carnegie, who funded the establishment of more than 2,500 libraries and gave away upward of $350 million prior to this death in 1919 famously stated, "The man who dies rich, dies disgraced."[10]

Andrew Carnegie believed in the transformative power of education. His foundation was initially known as The Carnegie Foundation for the Advancement of Teaching, chartered in 1906. While serving as a trustee of Cornell University, Carnegie became aware of the low pay and dismal retirement conditions of most university professors. His foundation served as a pension fund for universities across North

America to enable career educators to retire with dignity and financial security. By 1918 the foundation spun off this pension fund to form the independent nonprofit TIAA-CREF, the largest retirement management system for educators in the world. His foundation has gone on to support projects that benefit teaching and learning in many forms.

John D. Rockefeller. Sr. followed Carnegie's example, creating in 1913 the second US philanthropic institution. By 1927 Rockefeller had made personal contributions to the foundation totaling more than $180 million, equal to $2.8 billion in current value. His foundation in its earliest days focused on public health, making its first grant to the American Red Cross. The Rockefeller Foundation went on to support domestic and international medical education, creating public health schools at Johns Hopkins and Harvard, then in Toronto, London, and Beijing. It has since broadened its scope of global impact to include investment in sustainable energy, arts education, and food insecurity.

While Henry Ford claimed to distrust "charity," he is credited with having given away 1/3 of his income by the time of his death in 1947, perhaps most notably funding the completion of the Henry Ford Hospital in Detroit, Michigan. It was his son, Edsel, who established the Ford Foundation with an initial bequest of $25,000 in 1936.[11] The foundation set out to use its funds to support "scientific, education and charitable purposes, all for the public welfare." With the deaths of both Henry and Edsel Ford in the 1940s, their bequests made the Ford Foundation the largest philanthropy in the world.[12]

Known more for his delicious products than for his philanthropy, Milton Hershey, founder of Hershey Chocolates, was another extremely wealthy individual committed to divesting himself of his fortune before his death. Hershey exemplified a businessman who invested in his local community, in essence building the town of Hershey, PA, from the ground up. His lasting legacy is the Milton Hershey School, originally established as a residential vocational school for orphan boys. Today the private school provides free residential education to about 2,000 boys and girls from around the United States each year.

Not surprisingly each of these names still lends gravitas to billion-dollar foundations that continue to be highly engaged, powerful players in philanthropy decades after the death of their namesakes.

Of course, in some cases these acts of generosity were forms of investment that facilitated the growth of markets and greater wealth for the benefactors. You might say that Henry Ford raised his workers' wages not out of philanthropy but from the recognition that enabling his workers to afford to buy a car expanded his market opportunity. Nonetheless, it's worth noting that at this time in American history, private individuals like these industrialists were funding projects that only later came to be considered the responsibility of the government like building bridges, schools, railroads, and highways.

In the aftermath of the Great Depression of 1929 under Franklin D. Roosevelt's leadership, government stepped in as a major investor, forming numerous programs like the TVA (Tennessee Valley Authority), the WPA (Works Progress Administration), and many others to create employment by building infrastructure. Over time the government replaced private philanthropy as the major funder for public works, a trend that continued until the 1980s when then President Ronald Reagan championed the downsizing of government spending on domestic social programs (more about this in Chapter 4). Philanthropy has not yet acted on the need to fill the gaps left by shrinking government investments in social well-being.

Not Your Grandfather's Philanthropy

I'm a numbers guy, so I want to restate some of the impressive figures mentioned earlier.

- ◆ 813 US billionaires currently (up from 66 billionaires in 1990)
- ◆ $5.4 trillion, the combined net worth of the 400 wealthiest Americans today

These staggering figures raise the obvious question. Where are the Carnegies, Rockefellers, and Fords for the twenty-first century? Some names do come to mind: Gates, Buffet, and Bloomberg. Each of these men has contributed billions of dollars of personal wealth[13] to their foundations to fund work for public benefit through causes they believe in, whether it's the environment, arts, government innovation, reproductive health, or the eradication of global disease. And there are some exciting emerging funders like Lauren Powell Jobs, Melinda Gates, and Mackenzie Scott showcasing the power of "trust-based" philanthropy (more about that later). But what we see far more frequently than acts of largesse for public benefit are acquisitions that extend the power and prestige of the uber-wealthy in the form of supersize yachts, pro sports teams, or missions to Mars. The real question though is if we are growing a wealthy class at a rapid rate (look at the previous data), why aren't we seeing a mirroring of that growth in the number of grant makers coming from this newfound wealth?

As a society we have replaced the expectation that the super-rich will make substantial financial gifts for the good of the general public with an attitude of awe and respect for their ability to accumulate unprecedented wealth. Instead of admiring them for building libraries, we admire them for building personal empires. This sector of philanthropy seems to have lost its way. But there is a proud and incredible history here, one that we can again embrace as Americans.

Within the circles of the super-rich a trend toward what has been dubbed "effective altruism" has begun to take hold. At its core, this multibillion-dollar movement applies business principles of optimization to the act of giving, expecting every donated dollar to do the best in measurable ways. But as *New York Times* business reporter Emma Goldberg pointed out in her piece entitled "What if Charity Shouldn't Be Optimized"[14], not only does this approach justify amassing outsize fortunes, even more unfortunately it limits the range of what causes and concerns merit philanthropic giving. Goldberg found that the desire for huge impact came at the expense of many small, community-based organizations that by their nature cannot deliver outsize impacts. Between 2010 and 2016, 20 million households stopped giving, putting charitable entities that depend on small-dollar donors in crisis. Perhaps too many of us have begun questioning the value of giving to a small arts organization or a restoration fund for a community landmark or an urban farmer training program. Do we think that Carnegie asked each of his libraries to submit annual reports on the number of books checked out or measure improvement in the grade levels of readers?

I am certainly not saying that measurement is irrelevant, but it has its place. A piece of your **portfolio of giving** should be dedicated to specific outcomes you hope to fund and generate. But we cannot imperil small nonprofits that serve immediate and pressing needs that are hard to quantify simply because we prefer to know the impact with certainty.

In particular, the effort to drive outcomes-based thinking has been long running in nonprofit circles. Impact Genome[15] in Chicago is attempting to define a taxonomy that will allow us to understand in more depth what the value of nonprofit work is. We cannot be fooled that this is the end of the crisis in society. We must ensure that these impact-denominated portfolio investments are augmented by other unrestricted funds along with infrastructure investments from government and targeted sector investments by aligned corporate entities.

Forms of Philanthropy

As our attitudes toward philanthropy have changed, so have the options available to institutional and individual donors. Private foundations, community foundations, donor-advised funds, family offices are all attracting donations. It's worth examining each of these options and their relationship to the stratification of wealth in the United States as we consider a new role for philanthropy.

PRIVATE FOUNDATIONS

Private foundations are perhaps the most familiar form of philanthropic giving. Foundations came into existence largely as a way for the ultra-wealthy to control where some of their fortunes would go and in the process avoid paying estate taxes. Essentially a solid tax dodge could double as a vehicle for public good and so these efforts were given the designation as 501(c)(3) tax-exempt entities by the Internal Revenue Service. To prevent the wealthy from simply tax-free sheltering money in their foundations to be spent by their families, Congress enacted legislation requiring 501(c)(3) organizations to annually grant 5% of their endowments to a public benefit through nonprofit entities.[16] Meanwhile the endowments would be allowed to grow, untaxed, through investment and additional contributions.

Today there are 10 or so enormous foundations such as the Gates Foundation, Open Society Foundation, Robert Wood Johnson Foundation, Rockefeller Foundation, Ford Foundation, and the Annie E. Casey Foundation and others whose endowments run to billions of dollars. These are robust, giant organizations that run very much like successful Fortune 500 companies. Historically these grantmaking organizations have defined missions and tend to focus on specific program areas.

Critics of traditional philanthropy have criticized large foundations for what they view as a paternalistic form of giving, involving grants with highly restricted uses and narrowly defined deliverables or "outputs." Similarly, critics have deep concerns for the inequitable systems with which these foundations select grantees and administer their funds and programs.

In 2020, largely in response to the murder of George Floyd and the rise of the Black Lives Matter movement, many more foundations turned their attention to more broadly defined concepts of social justice and racial equity. It was an impressive move into bold areas of social impact, but within a few years this support, and the grants that came with it, have waned. Pushback against diversity, equity, and inclusion (DEI) initiatives seems to have had a chilling effect on some foundations as they have quietly withdrawn support for on-the-ground efforts to effect social change. The liberal avant-garde had a good idea but cowered under criticism.

More encouragingly a new class of philanthropists is breaking the paternalistic, prescriptive mold by engaging in "trust-based" giving. Previously grantors often took a paternal approach, warning grant recipients that if they did not "deliver" specific results they would be denied any future funding. Nonprofit leaders began saying to grant makers "you're tying up money so much I can't do what I need to do to get this work done." They were asking for more unrestricted funds and "trust," based on their record as mature organizations with professional management and practices in place. Every hour they spent "complying" was a precious hour they were not spending on making their communities stronger.

As we mentioned, Melinda French Gates, Laurene Powell Jobs, and Mackenzie Scott have all pledged to give away billions to organizations working in areas they deem important. Instead of making many small, time-limited grants to multiple groups, they are awarding very large grants to a few entities on the basis of their past work, with few or no strings attached, not necessarily demanding certain measurable outcomes. The recipients are able to apply the money where it is needed to support their efforts. Trust-based giving helps remove the curse of starved overhead that cripples so many nonprofits. Donors typically want their dollars to go directly to those being served via programs and are unwilling to provide funding to "keep the lights on" or hire and fairly compensate nonprofit leadership and staff. Artificially suppressing reasonable investment in staff and facilities too often leads to burnout and ultimately the failure of a nonprofit. About three-quarters of surveyed leaders indicate that burnout among their staff is at least slightly impacting their organization's ability to achieve its mission.[17] Trust-based giving is a promising new approach that may ripple out to alter the relationships between grantors and grantees in a mutually beneficial way.

COMMUNITY FOUNDATIONS

These organizations are regionally oriented, and many major cities have one. Community Foundations are usually 501(c)(3) nonprofits with the mission of serving a public purpose. They act as a clearinghouse for philanthropy within a particular region. Community foundations are generally able to raise money to support various local nonprofit efforts by encouraging donations from residents who trust the foundation to put their tax-deductible contribution to good use. They create large pools of money and maintain relationships with donors and grantees to collect and direct money to benefit their resident population.

Unlike private foundations, community foundations have no mandate to donate 5% of holdings on a yearly basis for some general public purpose. Because they raise money from a diverse pool of entities and individuals, each of which may have differing goals for their money, they are not obliged to grant any certain amount. In practice, many of these foundations do utilize the 5% "rule" as a guidepost for their endowments. However some innovative community foundations such as the Greater Milwaukee Foundation have started campaigns to raise money for a better Greater Milwaukee but also for specific areas of need such as health equity, economic opportunity, housing security, and educational opportunity.[18] They are testing this approach for its measurable impact rather than continuing to adhere to any perceived or real limit on grantmaking or simply adding to their already significant endowment of ~$1.2 billion. This is an exciting way to see more robust outcomes achieved locally by encouraging larger infusions of cash resources to worthy nonprofits. Their cause-specific initiatives have also helped to significantly broaden their donor base.

DONOR-ADVISED FUNDS

Earlier I mentioned the stratification of wealth in the United States over the past few decades. Donor-advised funds (DAFs) are one example of how families at various levels of income can enjoy the tax advantages of the uber-wealthy without the same level of wealth.

DAFs have been around since the first one was created by the New York City Community Trust in 1931. But starting around 2015, DAFs became the fastest growing vehicle for charitable giving in the United States,[19] with an estimated $78 billion in assets held in nearly 27,000 accounts. Why? Because whether your fortune is in the billions, more than 100 million, between 10 and 100 million, or between 1 and 10 million, you can contribute to a donor-advised fund. Anywhere along the stratification of wealth, you can act like a mogul and derive the tax benefits.

Contributing to a DAF means surrendering control of your cash, securities, or other assets while retaining the ability to direct where your money goes and enjoying an immediate tax deduction. In addition, your contribution can be invested for tax-free growth, giving you additional funds for future giving. There is no IRS requirement for a certain percentage of annual giving from the DAF. It would be interesting for Congress to consider placing a granting requirement upon the positive tax treatment they have already applied to this nearly $80 billion.

The money management behemoth, Fidelity, manages one of the world's largest DAFs through its Fidelity Charitable arm. In 2023 alone its grants grew by more than $500,000,000 over 2022. In short, DAFs represent a vast ocean of uncoordinated wealth and giving potential.

FAMILY OFFICES

Even less coordinated and certainly less transparent are family offices. These are small organizations, often run by a direct family member, created by very wealthy individuals and enabling them to make grants of any amount for a special purpose. These offices commonly are not nonprofit organizations. Although they may chiefly serve to direct wealth advisory, they do regularly make grants to a variety of organizations focused on the public good. Generally, these entities operate with extremely low overhead, staffed sometimes with at most a few folks managing them. Family offices may be "evergreen" organizations if they have especially large endowments in excess of $100 million or if they impose strict constraints on giving to preserve capital and extend the life of the organization, sometimes in perpetuity.

Some family offices identify a specific cause and decide to deplete or "sunset" their funds to have the greatest impact. More typically though these legacy institutions keep a very low profile and aspire to operate largely anonymously. Typically, unlike foundations, they do not solicit applications from nonprofits, preferring to identify what they deem to be worthy organizations and approach the entities' leadership as possible recipients. The rule book for family offices tends not to be as defined as ones governing the other institutional forms of philanthropy. This lack of formal requirements allows family offices to operate quite independently. The untold millions or even billions of dollars held in family offices is another form of "disorganized" philanthropic dollars that probably is not achieving its full potential for delivering maximum public benefit. And family offices are most certainly not acting in concert with the other forces.

Challenges to Philanthropic Impact

Too often what discourages us from tackling systemic social problems is what we imagine will be prohibitive cost. Yes, correcting for decades of neglect and disinvestment will require huge investment. But how steep are the costs of continuing to do too little?

What I am suggesting is the direct opposite of "throwing money" at a problem. All too often we have seen the disappointing results of such a naïve, scattershot approach. When you consider the cumulative trillions of dollars the entire philanthropic sector holds, it's obvious our society has the money. And I believe we also have a sufficient number of individuals and institutions who want to redress past wrongs and rebuild communities. In Part 2 of this book, I'll lay out a more complete road map for effective change, but here are some approaches that, if implemented, can begin to harness more of the untapped power inherent in philanthropic entities.

CLARIFY AND EXPAND THE 5% "RULE"

As previously mentioned, what began as an IRS regulation imposed on most private foundations to ensure they were not simply a tax shelter for the wealthy has over time become misinterpreted as an inflexible limit to granting. Since endowments are affected by the rise and fall of institutional investments, adherence to a 5% limit means fluctuations, sometimes significant, in the amount of grants awarded. The upside can be great when markets and endowment balances rise while the downside can be little short of disastrous for small nonprofits.

While preservation of capital is a reasonable concern for foundations, adopting a less restrictive approach to available funds would make a big difference to the nonprofits that depend on foundation funding. Especially in times of governmental disinvestment, foundations need to understand that spending well beyond 5% is what society needs. Rebalancing their portfolios and replenishing their endowments can wait.

RECONSTRUCT LIMITATIONS TO BORROWING

Wealthy individuals and prosperous businesses routinely "leverage" their assets to borrow money. Despite having millions or even billions in their endowments, philanthropic institutions are sometimes prohibited from exercising this standard practice. When donors have permanently restricted the use of their contributions to endowments, a foundation cannot utilize any of the endowment's principal as leverage for a loan.[20] The adoption of the Uniform Prudent Management of Institutional Funds Act (UPMIFA) in nearly all of the states creates a myriad of complexities standing in the way of anyone with an endowment, especially when they are trying to unlock capital through leverage of endowed assets.[21]

DESIGN FOR IMPACTS, NOT OUTPUTS
In an effort to be able to show their money is making a difference, some philanthropies have asked for measurable deliverables. There's nothing wrong with that, except when the elements being measured don't amount to real impact. It can be the difference between using funds to "hire five individuals" or using those same funds to "decrease food insecurity in Chicago by 20%." Funders who design their giving for impact over outputs are more likely to change the status quo. As nonprofits see impact orientation as a way to unlock foundation dollars, they will also be able to communicate with other sources of capital using a language that makes sense to them. When nonprofits start showing how dollars spent result in specific outcomes, many more funders will believe their money is well invested. (We'll take a closer look at impact orientation in the next chapter.)

BECOME COMFORTABLE WITH SUNSETTING
Creating a legacy is a powerful motivator, so wanting to attach your family name to a foundation or cause is a very human impulse. However, to keep the legacy alive, capital must be preserved and granting limited (see 5% rule). We are beginning to see some individuals and some institutions commit to spending down their funds to achieve greater impact sooner. As wealth continues to be created in the private sector, we can replace the spent down dollars over time, putting much more capital directly to work on the problems inside our communities.

IMPROVE COORDINATION AMONG THE COMMUNITY
Philanthropy is a huge and frankly competitive industry. Cooperation and collaboration do not come naturally in a competitive environment where contributors and causes can be jealously guarded. Unlike a corporate free marketplace, there is ample room for coordination and collaboration when it comes to aligning resources—both knowledge-based and financial—around a common problem. Pooling of assets and efforts would amplify impact.

CHANGE UBER-WEALTHY "INTERFERENCE"
Going back to the examples of Carnegie, Ford, Rockefeller, and Hershey we see men who were brilliant innovators in business and

were almost unbelievably successful. To each of them, though, they did not believe their business acumen translated into excelling in every other field. They did not seek to practice medicine, or cure disease, or teach orphan children, or run the government. They sought out experts in all of those fields and invested in their efforts. Today we see our current "titans" of industry expressing confidence that they can apply their business skills to any social problem and "fix it." It is a level of arrogance and privilege previous twentieth-century philanthropists would at best have found puzzling. Billionaires have a role to play and if they get it right they can help, but not as the star performer.

CREATE PERSONAL IMPACT PORTFOLIOS

Some of the changes I advocate for are regulatory, some are questions of a changing mindset, and all are aimed at the philanthropic industry. But for individuals, there is also a powerful change we can adopt. Just as many of us are fortunate enough to have a financial portfolio, we should commit to investing in and managing a portfolio of giving. For example, my financial portfolio might consist of stocks, bonds, cash, bitcoin, annuities, and insurance. Our portfolio of giving should support a similarly diversified range of organizations and institutions that have meaning for us. Let's pledge to give to philanthropic efforts that offer measurable outcomes but also support some magnificent impact investments that defy measurement, like social justice. Things we may not see change in our lifetime, but in supporting them we join a long history of like-minded people committing to the long, slow journey of creating an equitable society.

Philanthropy and AI

Despite some of the criticisms I have of how philanthropy currently operates, those participating in philanthropy have several positive aspects to them that could make them major players in Artificial Intelligence. First, they stand as highly credible actors in setting up systems that address the challenges involved with building strong communities. Second, they have an enormous amount of convening power that could be leveraged in the newest areas of AI development.

The current versions of AI dominant in the world are the generative AI tools we have all become accustomed to—Open AI's ChatGPT, Google's Gemini, and others. The challenge is that these systems don't scale affordably, and while early access to these tools is impressive, the real value comes from sustained and coordinated large-scale use.

Luckily there are firms working now to lower the total cost of ownership of AI systems. MiPhi, for instance, is a joint venture in India designed specifically to make the incredible power of AI accessible to the masses, including companies, governments, universities, and nonprofits.[22] Foundations can serve as powerful hubs in this new version of AI as it is deployed. Each region will need trusted parties to convene others together and coordinate in a private, secure, and scalable way. This new technology can be brought to bear affordably by regionally powerful foundations for use by the community. And the power of training coming from every community to new models will be unstoppable.

Summary and What's Ahead

In this chapter we have learned in depth about the current status and nature of philanthropy and foundations in America as well as the history of the philanthropic sector. We have explored some of the specific challenges in front of foundations and philanthropists as well as concrete examples of change in policy and processes to make sure that this force can be truly successful in their stated goals.

In the upcoming chapters, I will continue to argue that as a society we need all four forces, namely philanthropy, nonprofits, business, and government to fix themselves first. The "fix" must include a recognition of their unique strengths along with fresh insights into how they may blend their resources and efforts to achieve a far greater positive impact than they currently attain. Success in this venture will require a deep focus on collaboration among the forces for the public good. In the next chapter, we'll take a look at the ecosystem of nonprofits, their constraints, and special strengths, along with suggestions for process improvement.

CHAPTER 3

Nonprofits Beyond the Soup Kitchen

"The world we're living in right now, at least in our own country, is that there's such disagreement about what the problem is or problems are. That makes it hard to work toward solutions . . . I think the failure to listen to the people who are experiencing what it is you're trying to fix is a big historical failure."

**—Ginny Finn, Chief Development Officer,
Milwaukee Area Technical College**

We've all done it. Made a side-by-side comparison of two products and bought the significantly cheaper one because, hey, how much different could the name brand be from the no-name version? What was it for you? Knock-off chicken soup that tasted like salt and chemicals? A stylish blouse that fell apart after one washing? Bargain airline tickets for a flight that was inconvenient, uncomfortable, and a lousy way to start a vacation? I'm not saying that the most expensive option is always better or even justifiable. But more often than not it is still true that you get what you pay for.

What does this have to do with nonprofits? Everything.

Collectively we have come to view many nonprofits as the "off brand" solution to social problems. Cheaper, not very attractively packaged, less efficient perhaps. The perception being that these are efforts run by good-hearted though possibly less capable people doing "good enough" work for the money we donate.

Over time the perception shapes the reality. Nonprofits largely have come to be defined by a scarcity mindset. They view themselves as undercapitalized, act as if they are and don't seem to plan to get themselves out of an annual dependence on asking for cash. In their well-intentioned efforts they don't provide themselves with the best resources possible but settle for whatever resources they can find. Many seem to have acquiesced to the common though perhaps unconscious belief that nonprofits don't deserve to have great marketing teams, or a polished social media presence. There's a sense that the leaders and workers in the nonprofit sector deserve to earn far less than their counterparts in corporate jobs. Their reward is the satisfaction of knowing they are doing meaningful work, not their paycheck. Typically, nonprofits spend too much of their time "making do" with too little: money, facilities, staff, support.

Misguided critics may point to a lack of outcomes achieved by nonprofits as justification for withholding additional resources. But the hard truth, as any for-profit successful leader can attest to, is that *by lowering our sights in what we accept we also lower our sights for what we can achieve.* Trap employees in a dingy, bare bones workplace, deprive them of the tools they need to be efficient, require them to take on multiple roles across the operation, foster a constant sense of precarity, that any day might be our last, and what result can you expect? The atmosphere in which people work becomes what they produce. To put it bluntly, an awful environment produces awful outcomes. Burnout, which is now dominant in the nonprofit sector,[1] is the inevitable consequence.

Without the sufficient amount of resources and capital, unless they demand the best instead of accepting whatever is available, nonprofits can never fully realize their potential as powerful agents of social change. And certainly, they cannot serve as solid replacements for services the more deeply resourced government once provided. "[We have] limited access to professional fundraising, marketing, tech, and financial management personnel," says one leader. "Our administrative team is stretched too thinly to be able to function at a high level in any one domain." Leaders who self-identify as people of color report that burnout is having a slightly greater impact on their organization's ability to achieve its mission than leaders who do not identify as people of color.[2]

As a society we need to work to eliminate the scarcity mentality holding nonprofits back and directly contributing to burnout. We saw in the last chapter that lack of capital isn't the problem. In the chapter on the corporate sector, we'll see that there's an abundance of available, highly skilled talent. But before we go to solutions, let's explore the history and current state of the nonprofit sector.

Powered by People

As the psychologist and author Mary Pipher celebrated in a recent essay, "The world is filled with helpers."[3] Her observation holds true throughout our history. Way back in 1831 the French sociologist and political theorist Alexis de Tocqueville wrote, "I must say that I have seen Americans make a great deal of real sacrifices to the public welfare; and have noticed a hundred instances in which they hardly ever failed to lend a faithful support to one another."

Going back to the 1700s, colonists formed volunteer-based organizations to serve their fledgling communities. At first their social impact mission may have been to address very localized needs, such as the volunteer fire company Benjamin Franklin founded in Philadelphia in 1736. The Union Fire Company was the first of its kind, a fully volunteer-operated entity focused on fighting urban fires. This model proved so successful that it soon spread to other cities and towns. Even today many small rural communities rely on volunteers to staff their fire stations.

Over time citizens began to establish volunteer-run organizations to address what they perceived to be larger social needs. One example of this is The Society for the Relief of Free Negroes Unlawfully Held in Bondage,[4] founded in 1775. This was one of the earliest abolitionist organizations in our history and it grew to become the Pennsylvania Abolition Society.

These are just two examples of the many social impact, volunteer-based entities from the eighteenth and early nineteenth centuries. The Peabody Education Fund,[5] founded in 1867, is generally recognized as the first "modern" nonprofit in the United States. Baltimore banker George Peabody endowed this foundation with $2.1 million with the mission to improve education for all children, regardless of race, in the post-Civil War South. Peabody's nonprofit represents the first major example of "long-distance philanthropy,"[6] under which a donor's dollars left their region to improve conditions in another geographic area of need. It was also among the first nonprofits of scale, a trend that accelerated during the so-called Progressive Era of US history, spanning roughly the 1890s through the 1920s. Nationwide scores of activists and community leaders embraced causes calling for social and political reforms and founded scalable nonprofits to address these concerns; Clara Barton founded the American Red Cross in Washington DC, the United Way was begun in Denver, and the first Community Foundation was established in Cleveland.

To Tax or Not to Tax

So, America generally has given rise to social support for pressing needs due to necessity. But is there more that we could do collectively? Today we commonly characterize nonprofits as being tax-exempt themselves while offering tax relief for wealthy donors. It may surprise you to learn that this was not always the case. In 1894, legislation was proposed to create tax exemptions for nonprofit organizations. The Wilson–Gorman Tariff Act passed into law that year but was later ruled unconstitutional by the US Supreme Court in 1895. Nonprofits were not granted tax-exempt status until the Revenue Act of 1909. Then it was not until the subsequent Revenue Act of 1917 that individuals could claim income tax deductions for their charitable gifts.

The next time legislation directly impacting nonprofit organizations was enacted followed the massive social changes spurred by the Civil Rights Movement and opposition to the Vietnam War in the 1960s. In 1969 the Tax Reform Act created the IRS Section 501(c)(3) code establishing guidelines by which organizations could gain tax-exempt status and also qualify as private foundations. Prior to this, charities could claim the status, but the IRS could contest their claim. By securing 501(c)(3) status, organizations were now also able to offer tax deductions to their donors. Consequently, the IRS experienced a significant uptick in the number of applications. As the nonprofit sector grew rapidly, so too did the amount of rules, regulations, and policies aimed at keeping tabs on this sector.

One final piece of relevant legislation is a bill passed by Congress in 1976 allowing nonprofits to spend up to $1 million annually on lobbying efforts. As we look at the interconnection of philanthropy, government, and business with the nonprofit sector, the importance of advocacy through lobbying will be a topic we will return to.

An unanticipated consequence of this multitude of regulations has been an accumulation of asset wealth within the sector. The IRS estimates that while expenses and revenues for these organizations has stayed largely on pace, the net assets inside these organizations across the country has grown unabated. From 1985 to 2004 alone, the net assets in public charities grew by more than 27%.[7]

Boom Times

Nonprofit organizations are almost always stood up as a direct response to some acute social pain as the history of the sector demonstrates. In the United States, we have commonly seen nonprofits form as government has stepped away from addressing or altogether avoided responding to certain societal needs. When political leaders threaten to, or actually do, shut down the government, the nonprofit sector has no choice but to backfill the gap.[8] Often when a gap appears in the social safety net, passionate, motivated individuals step up to fill the hole, acting more from immediate necessity than from planned organizational design and strategy.

Forming a new nonprofit carries very low overhead and is hampered by little to no governing process within its community. This lack of what in business is referred to as significant "barriers to entry" enables individuals to move quickly to propose a social solution. But it can also contribute to a proliferation of similar entities and a duplication of efforts. It's not at all unusual to find multiple very small nonprofits attempting to operate within the same geography, most likely targeting a similar pool of potential funders and donors for contributions. Within the donor class this overlap tends to create cynicism captured in the not very flattering metaphor comparing small nonprofits to lobsters in a bucket, clawing and climbing over each other to get to scarce resources. Studies have shown that mergers of similarly situated nonprofit organizations can be successful and push forward an efficient use of resources in a cause area.[9]

In 1998 there were just more than 1 million nonprofits operating in the United States.[10] As of 2023, that number had jumped to 2 million, though more than 1 million of these entities reported operating revenues less than $50,000.[11] A woefully small amount of capital and an indication of how precarious many nonprofits are. The 2023 Statista report ranks the challenges nonprofits acknowledge facing. Rising operating expenses, lack of financial resources, insufficient staff capacity, and difficulty recruiting and retaining staff top the (long) list of impediments to accomplishing their missions.

Imagine if you were trying to establish and grow a business with this many constraints. You'd probably decide the effort simply wasn't worth it. Yet there can be no doubt our society needs stable, effective nonprofit organizations. Why will we always need them? Because society, unlike successful corporations, is inefficient by default though not necessarily by purposeful action. Society will inevitably create unfair results. But that doesn't mean we can't organize efforts to mitigate these outcomes. Fortunately, people are inspired to stand up and correct these inequities. Often they believe their best solution at hand is to form a nonprofit, though their path to financial viability is too frequently unclear or even unlikely. Collaboration many times is an afterthought.

Nonprofits as Value Creators

It's been said that the only difference separating the way a successful for-profit entity operates from nonprofit management is their tax return. I'd agree that excellent leadership, adherence to strong core values, a clear mission, a commitment to superior products, and customer service are some of the traits corporations and nonprofits should share. But their measures for success couldn't be more disparate.

Corporate performance depends on a healthy bottom line and the continuous creation of shareholder value. Companies work hard to distinguish themselves in the marketplace, identifying their competitive advantage and fiercely competing to preserve or grow their market share and quash their rivals. Continuous growth is the mantra of capitalism. Bigger is nearly always considered better.

The bottom line for nonprofits is to deliver value to society by solving or at least lessening a social need, whether that means filling gaps in health care, food access, education, housing, addiction recovery, or a host of other issues. These efforts don't make money. They cost money. For-profit enterprises earn money by selling to customers. Nonprofits' "customers" are generally not in a position to pay for the services they receive. Operating revenue must come from another set of "customers" in the form of funders, donors, and grants. For too long, the metrics used to determine whether a nonprofit is "successful" or "deserving" have focused less on impact, or outcomes, and more on a set of assumptions that trap nonprofits in cycles of scarcity and underperformance—or worse, lead to mismanagement, deception, and even embezzlement.

We have too narrowly been calculating the so-called return on investment (ROI) of nonprofits' work and in so doing are missing the much greater financial impact and value creation they alone can generate.

Here are some numbers that may surprise you:

◆ Covering the variety of costs nonprofits incur to run their operations, e.g., rent, utilities, office supplies, etc., is estimated to pump about **$1 trillion** into the national economy annually.[12]
◆ Nonprofits employ about 10% of the US workforce and are our third largest employer after retail and manufacturing,[13] annually paying more than **$800 billion** in salaries, benefits, and payroll taxes.
◆ In 2021, **56%** of Americans made a donation to a nonprofit organization.[14]
◆ In 2023 combined donations from individuals, bequests, foundations, and corporations reached an estimated **$557.16 billion**.[15] It's worth noting that giving from individuals outpaced all other contributors.

While these figures may be larger than you imagined, I'm guessing you'll be even more surprised by the value contributed by volunteers. A survey conducted by AmeriCorps and the US Census Bureau discovered that in 2023 alone **73 million** people, 28% of all Americans, gave of their time to support nonprofits. This represents a substantial increase from the 60 million volunteers counted in 2021. In the words of AmeriCorps CEO, Michael Smith, "We are witnessing a remarkable resurgence in volunteering. By focusing on impact rather than just counting hours of service, we are closing the gap between those in need and the support they deserve."

If we did the accounting for the estimated 4.99 billion hours of volunteer service in 2023, we'd arrive at the impressive sum of $167 billion of "free" labor. We're not just talking about filling bags with food at pantries or repairing bikes, though these are extremely valuable services. There are also countless highly skilled professionals such as coders or architects, lawyers, social media marketers, and many other disciplines willing to donate their expertise to advance the work of nonprofits whose mission they share. One advantage of modern technology is the opportunity for "virtual" volunteer work to occur off-site. The AmeriCorps survey found that between September 2022 and September 2023, an impressive 13.4 million people participated in virtual or hybrid volunteering, averaging 95 hours of service in that period. I can tell you from my time as CEO of Catchafire, Inc., the world's largest skills-based volunteering system, the interest in skills-based volunteering is significantly on the rise.

It's my belief that even nonprofits who rely on volunteers don't fully recognize the value or harness the full potential of volunteerism. Volunteers should be considered part of an organization's infrastructure. That's how essential they are. They're so much more than "nice to have" and they deserve to be invested in by nonprofits just as they invest in technology and facilities. The second hire an executive director should make is not a director of development; it's a highly skilled director of volunteers.

Before we move off the topic of value and volunteers specifically, it may also surprise you to know that youth, not retirees, make up the largest percentage of volunteers. I find it heartening to see that between 2019–2021 young people aged 16–17 had the highest volunteer rate of all age groups at 28%. Next in line were adults, most frequently parents, aged 45–54.[16] Generation X adults (currently aged 43–58) had the highest rate of volunteerism of any of the generational cohorts.

This level of engagement among youth and Gen X suggests that volunteering can be a lifelong commitment, providing invaluable support for nonprofits. Even more importantly, volunteering builds communities by fostering greater understanding, connection, empathy, a sense of purpose and empowerment—all traits that provide a strong foundation for thriving neighborhoods and societies.

What Is Limiting Nonprofit Success?

In a word, the chief challenge holding back nonprofits is distribution. I'm hesitant to use this word because it is more often associated with supply chains and with goods more than services. However, in the nonprofit sector—and this extends to their funders as well—open and transparent communication and collaboration about the issues and interventions each party is engaged in is by far still the exception and not the rule. This lack of collaboration results in an uneven and suboptimal distribution of resources of all sorts: time, talent, and money.

In my Milwaukee community, for example, there are more than 10 nonprofits focusing on aspects of racial equity on the north side of the city. Practically speaking, this means multiple dedicated, serious-minded organizations are competing for a limited pool of funds from, most likely, the identical set of potential individual and institutional funders and government programs. Imagine how much more these parties would be able to affect if, instead of competing for dollars while providing overlapping services, they were combining and coordinating their specific skills and resources. Such a consolidation of mission-driven organizations would bring much more firepower to the problems at hand. And collaboration does not mean canceling a particular set of services. Organizations dedicated to supporting a vibrant Black arts program as well as developing Black leadership, for example, can work side by side, sharing their common expenses and together generating greater impact toward improving racial equity in the city.

When I talk about distribution, it is intended to signal a fundamental change in the way nonprofits operate. Some of this is bound to be painful, but it should also be liberating. I'm calling for nonprofits to capitalize on a key difference separating them from for-profit enterprises. The success of for-profits requires successful competition. You have to distinguish yourself from others in your space and beat them in the contest for market dominance. Collaboration within the various sectors of for-profit industry is virtually unheard of. When nonprofits mimic this competitive, "crush the enemy" corporate mentality, they consign themselves to that "lobsters in a bucket" scenario of too many players scrabbling to acquire their share of too few resources. Over and over again.

Nonprofits exist in a world of higher callings and markedly different outcomes than corporate's laser focus on building shareholder value and a fat bottom line. Mimicking corporate tactics is a tragic mistake. What if those remarkable people who are inspired to tackle a pressing injustice got together with other like-minded organizations to map out a new distribution method? My guess is that they could build a new distribution model that provides a well-defined, nonduplicative role for every player and every dollar. Imagine how funders and communities would respond to a road map for greater impact at the same or even less cost.

The first step toward repositioning distribution demands some serious soul-searching. Existing nonprofits would be compelled to kill some programs they wish they could hold onto, mainly in instances where someone else has a better, stronger, proven intervention already in place. An honest assessment of where the coverage is and where the gaps linger would enable both service providers and nonprofit investors to identify and target where their efforts and money can have the greatest chance for success. Sometimes this will mean a nonprofit should merge with another entity or even close its doors because it is unable to serve its mission effectively. This is a non-narcissistic version of taking care of your community. Targeted outcomes are not about feeling good for making an effort. Outcomes are solely focused on measurably improving life across the community, not tied to founder or funder ego or public image.

Examining and eventually restructuring distribution in the nonprofit sector can and should be practiced at every level of engagement: local, regional, and national. The objective should be to eliminate over-covering and wasted resources, both human and financial. Instead of a top-down organization taking on this process, a bottom-up effort of regions getting together on their own and identifying the work that needs to be done promises more likelihood of sustainable practice. These efforts are not just about sunsetting duplicate services. They also enable sharing costs on common concerns. Having a shared services model for things like technology, human resources, creative marketing, and other expense line items would allow for a vibrant community of professionals working toward one goal, pursued through multiple avenues.

Although I'm advocating that nonprofits thrive when they don't imitate for-profit operations, there is one corporate model that may prove very useful in an effort to rebuild an impactful distribution system. Enterprise architecture is an approach by which companies set up a standard framework used to guide the process of assessing where true need/opportunity exists and where work is already happening. It may take an institutional funder or a well-established nonprofit to lead this process, convening local and regional nonprofits to both contribute to the findings and consent to be guided by the resulting report. Being able to provide such objective, accurate data to potential funders and investors equips participating nonprofits with a far more compelling "ask." Their request for funding is tied to their unique, valuable contribution to a coordinated effort that promises to fill a crucial gap in their operation as part of a larger collaboration. By continually publishing such a comprehensive report, the donor community can quickly identify funding gaps in the overall cause area and more effectively direct their dollars as needs evolve.

The Alignment of Need with Opportunity

Throughout our history we've gone through periods of waxing and waning equity. Coming out of the widespread hardships brought on by the Great Depression and World War II, the federal government stepped up with massive social impact interventions. The introduction of New Deal era programs created opportunities for a new workforce coming back from war, industrial growth happening at large scale, greatly expanded access to higher education and home ownership—all of which contributed to the rapid rise of a prosperous middle class, albeit one that still favored white citizens.

Throughout the 1940s and 1950s the federal government embarked on unprecedented levels of investment in infrastructure, building interstate highways, bridges, and schools funded through appropriate levels of taxation. Corporations stepped up to contribute to industrial growth by providing employment along with benefits of health care coverage and pensions that provided crucial eleents of a social safety net. The combined commitments and investments of government and corporations enabled millions of US citizens to get back on their feet after the devastation of the 1920s and 1930s. There was a pervasive sense that "we're all in this together," an attitude we seem to have lost over the past few decades. We find ourselves now in a period more defined by divisiveness than by inclusion. We seem to have lost the recognition that we are and always will be in this society together.

Corporations primarily respond to shareholder demands for profitable growth. Meanwhile government at all levels continues to be challenged to do more with less as a tolerance for taxation and regulation recedes. These transitions appear to be less than conscious. There was never a time when we collectively decided that business should stop providing for the welfare of its employees or that government should dismantle the social safety net. Yet here we are, at a time when it appears that no one is advocating for the coordination of the four forces (philanthropy, nonprofits, government, and business) that has always supported this country. It is not the case that people don't believe in supporting their neighbors. Americans are legendary for their generosity in response to crises and disasters across the nation. The steady decline of support across all four forces is veiled and simply not called out or part of our public discourse. I want us to pay attention to the extent of the society's needs again, as we have done historically, and urge all institutions to stand up together to fill the void we are facing. America's greatness has always been most evident when we align behind a common cause.

When government and corporations retreat, the demand curve for social services invariably rises. In this period of uncertainty brought on by significant shifts in social and political trends, we are facing an even greater need for the "on the ground" interventions nonprofits are uniquely positioned to deliver. The time is now to help nonprofits find their way to change and come to a better solution for meeting expanding needs.

My work has shown me that hope for a better society has not died, all the bleak news to the contrary. Hope and determination still live in the space we're talking about—among corporate leaders, philanthropists, government leaders, and bureaucrats, and those extraordinary people dedicating their undercompensated and underappreciated talents to nonprofits. We don't need everyone to get behind this idea of radical collaboration. If only a core set of people on the left and right can get together it would start a next wave of social impact, repositioning their efforts not as "stand alone do-gooders" but as partners in building a more equitable society. We might think of this new era as a time for leaders to be Social Industrialists, rebuilding a more just society.

The need for equity never goes away, but as our history shows it is shouldered by different organizations at different times. The broad shoulders necessary to bring about social justice can be formed only when the effort is shared equitably among the four forces: philanthropy, nonprofits, government, and corporations.

Nonprofits and AI

There certainly is much that needs to be shouldered by the nonprofit community. And resources, as stated in this chapter, are often scarce and hard to come by. But the one thing that every nonprofit has whether they realize it or not, is data. AI lives off of data to train the models so that they are able to make accurate inferences and help guide progress. Nonprofits sit on tons of data that could be analyzed as a whole making societal gains much simpler. For instance, nonprofits need to fill out multiple IRS forms (990s and others). They fill out applications and reports to foundations. They produce annual reports for their boards. They produce multiple documents annually that characterize the problems they address in order to raise funds. All of these data sources can be fed into an affordable AI solution as I have talked about before. And while they secure that data and analysis in trusted regional systems, ultimately these insights can be shared in a large language model that can be pointed at sharing common solutions derived by AI and delivered by the sharing of this mass of data from nonprofits throughout the country. This will need to happen in a local manner and with affordable and easily scalable solutions. The cloud-only approach to AI won't work. But as stated earlier, industry is working to solve that problem. And now nonprofits can be the source of data.

Summary and What's Ahead

In this chapter we deeply started to understand nonprofits—their challenges and their goals. We started by understanding the scarcity mindset and its impact on nonprofits. We discussed the birth of and history of nonprofits in the country. We now understand the depths of the challenges they face but also the incredible value they drive and the limits society places on them. We ended by discussing how we can leverage the power of AI to unleash the incredible outcomes nonprofits hope to achieve.

In the next chapter we will see how governments of all levels have similar and sometimes different impacts on strengthening communities.

CHAPTER 4

Government for the People

"One avenue that is really helpful and impactful is for local governments to reach out to philanthropic opportunities within those communities to help support, not 100%, but to help support in a 50/50 partnership model."

—Deb Fowler, Executive Director,
History UnErased

The Francis Scott Key Bridge collapses in Baltimore Harbor. Hurricane Helene dumps 30 inches of rain on Asheville, North Carolina. Wildfires obliterate large swaths of Los Angeles. Who you gonna call?

In times of natural disasters, major catastrophes, and large-scale disruptions we all turn to the government. Every single time. Even the folks who claim to resent or even hate "the Feds" recognize how limited their options are and how insufficient their resources are without government intervention and assistance. It's not just about the money either, but the manpower and the expertise government officials and employees can bring to bear.

We all count on government at every level, local, state, regional, and federal, to be there in a crisis. But an effective system of governance needs to deliver far more than emergency management systems on demand. Citizens and government leaders must shift their perception of what government can, should, and indeed must do.

Instead of relying on government as a "vending machine of service delivery," a collaborative shift at all levels of society has to occur. We have the power to support a transformation of government, enabling our public servants and elected officials to think of themselves as platform builders and maintainers. Citizens can look to government to act as a powerful co-creator of solutions with widespread positive social impact, a far more constructive role than they are currently able to fill.

That may sound far-fetched, implausible, or even impossible, but I'm not the first (or hopefully the last) to see the corrective measures necessary to reposition and reinvigorate government. Before we go to solutions, let's trace the historic trends and various forms of disruption that have contributed to the perceived erosion of our government's problem-solving ability.

Downgrading the Government's Report Card

In Chapter 1, I cited the dramatic decline in Americans' belief in the efficiency and effectiveness of their government, a score plummeting from an overall approval rating of 77% in 1964 to a dismal 20% by 2020. In 2022 the Partnership for Public Trust began surveying the US population to measure their level of confidence in the federal government. In just two years, their research found that the already low trust score of 35% sank to 23%.[1] This decline is agnostic. The numbers stay constant across demographic groups without significant variation due to race, ethnicity, gender, age, political affiliation, and education level. Sadly, we may have found one thing 8 out of 10 Americans agree on—the federal government sucks.

As of 2022, Pew Research discovered that only about 24% of Americans believe the government has done a good job managing immigration or lifting people out of poverty. And even as inflation eased and the US economy's recovery from the COVID-19 pandemic was the envy of the developed world, posting much stronger GDP growth than any other economy, Americans downgraded their faith in the government's ability to foster a strong economy. In 2020 that rating was 54%. By 2022 the number slumped to 37%. In contrast the Feds still earn high marks for responding to natural disasters and preventing terrorist acts (70% and 68% respectively), although we will see how the current underinvestment in FEMA impacts this traditionally strong score.[2]

Under Presidents Ronald Reagan and Bill Clinton surveys indicated short-lived reversals of the downward trend, with some upticks in hope, confidence, and trust in government. Reagan spoke of hope and honor, offering a begrudging acceptance of bipartisanship. Clinton brought in a more youthful energy with a vision of hope, growth, and a nod to social justice. Neither of these increases in belief in government lasted past either president's time in office.

Worse than the short-term impacts of false hopes or failed agendas, I contend that Ronald Reagan continually thrust the dagger into public trust beginning with his 1981 inauguration speech. Reagan lit the match that served as accelerant to the decline in trust that began in the 1960s. And the skepticism and cynicism he fostered was not limited to the federal government. After the scientific triumphs of the 1960s, most notably the United States being the first to land a man on the moon, Reagan called into question the credibility of science especially related to the environment. It's a short line from his disparaging remarks to the dismissal of medical experts during the COVID-19 pandemic and the rise of Climate Deniers.[3]

The sobering truth about grading government performance reveals a story of steady, even precipitous, decline. There is, however, a modicum of good news. Americans' faith in government is lowest at the national level, a bit stronger at the state level, and higher still at the local level.[4] This finding calls to mind another of Alexis de Tocqueville's prescient observations about American democracy.

"Municipal institutions are to liberty what primary schools are to science; they place it within reach of the people, they teach men to use it and to enjoy it. A nation may establish a free government, but without municipal institutions it cannot have the spirit of liberty."

What Went Wrong

My analysis of the supporting data suggests three successive turning points in public trust and faith in government since the 1960s.

- ◆ **Civil Rights and Flower Power in the 1960s:** First, the extremely high level of support in the early 1960s appears to significantly suffer and never heal from the social upheavals of race; the assassinations of President John Kennedy, civil rights leader Martin Luther King, Jr., and Senator Robert Kennedy; anti-war tensions and demonstrations; and the generational stresses between The Greatest Generation and the hippie Flower Power movement spanning the mid to late 1960s.

- ◆ **Government failures in the 1980s and 1990s:** This was followed by two successive efforts at engendering and losing hope by half of the population as we lived through polar opposite swings from Reagan Republicans to Clinton Democrats. Partisan shifts in the presidency have had deleterious effects on trust in the relevant party when all that was promised did not come to pass. Such shortfalls of government leaders failing to deliver on their promised vision results in pulling the whole country's beliefs down. No party is immune from deeply disappointing its constituents.

- ◆ **A global pandemic and racial upheaval in the 2000s:** Much remains to be studied and understood about the implications resulting from the cascade of crises during 2019–2020 or what some people refer to as "The Before Times." The National Library of Medicine shared a study exploring some key factors negatively affecting public trust. The study cites several major events.
  - The COVID-19 pandemic inducing widespread panic, as well as social and economic disruptions.
  - George Floyd's murder and the rise of the Black Lives Matter movement prompting divisive stances on policing.
  - The dramatic rise in race-related hate crimes, some triggered by blaming Asia for the pandemic.
  - A tragic spike in urban gun violence and a 30% increase in the national murder rate.[5]

This study points to the correlation between the erosion of trust in government with its increasing inability to govern.[6] The seemingly instant access to a global wealth of information and its unbelievably fast acceleration caused by the creation of multiple viral social media platforms during this time frame created the environment for a shocking loss of public trust.

The major change we're experiencing in the public's perception of government now seems to be that members of both major political parties are significantly disenchanted across multiple cause areas. Voters from either party may not agree on the same solutions, but they are registering their joint frustration with government's inability to correct what they view as troubling and critical issues such as uncontrolled immigration and a lack of economic opportunity.

Why Trust Matters

Picture yourself facing an unfamiliar decision. You have a choice to make: do this or do that; take this or take that; go here or stay away. How do you decide? Yes, there's Google, more recently AI and ChatGPT, and reams of available "advice" via social media, but how do you know what's right for you? Most of us will defer to the sources we trust most. No matter how savvy or highly educated or experienced we are, it's impossible to know the best action to take at every life challenge. It's natural to seek a trusted person, organization, or institution. A high level of trust often gives us the confidence we need to choose. Many of us encounter this situation in matters of personal health when we rely on a physician who has earned our trust.

Trust is a feeling that's hard to measure, but as it turns out it has been for some time an area of interest not just to social scientists but to economists. Their findings point to a strong correlation between the general level of trust and the efficacy of the government, especially in a democracy. Surprising? Not when you consider how much of civil society rests on our overall willingness to comply willingly with a complex system of rules and regulations. We can't claim to know how we should act in every situation and historically we have trusted in a range of institutions to provide guidance, including the government.

We don't need to look further than the varied responses to the COVID-19 pandemic to find examples of how broken our system of trust has become. In a 2023 study shared by the National Center for Biotechnology Information's National Library of Medicine,[7] the authors report that "economic, social, and political anxieties pervasive through-out the pandemic influenced trust in the United States government." Specifically, the erosion or even destruction of trust in other institutions has had a rippling impact on the ability of government to achieve broad levels of compliance. From the ideological left's increasing lack of belief in the police to the right's distrust of the Centers for Disease Control and Prevention (CDC) as an institution, distrust of many aspects of government appears far more widespread than the cyclical political skepticism or cynicism driven by presidential party politics. We see evidence of diminishing compliance in the sharp decline of children's vaccination rates, the pushback on guidelines for COVID-19 shutdowns and protocols, and the challenging of numerous other social norms.

Watching the economist and policymaker Sir Timothy Besley's hour-long presentation on his research is probably more of a commit-ment than you're willing to make. But if you are willing, this is a fasci-nating, complex, and interdisciplinary deep dive into the role trust plays in the public sphere. One of his chief conclusions is that "trust building is a key part of building peace and prosperity."[8] These highly desirable outcomes are more likely to be accomplished by increasing the effec-tiveness of the state.

Besley's research spans decades as does Rebecca Cohen's article, "Breaking down public trust."[9] Cohen points to critical junctures in US history from the anti-war protests of the 1960s through the Watergate exposé, the oil embargo of the 1970s, and Ronald Reagan's oft-quoted 1981 inaugural address in which he won applause for his comment that "Government is not the solution to our problem, government is the problem." The Pew Research Center noticed a slight increase in trust in the US government post the 9/11 attacks, but overall the level of trust has been in decline for decades.

Combining these studies with even a casual reading of recent news reports shows me that there is not only a demonstrable and impactful decrease in trust, but also that there is a broad base of issues driving mistrust. While some meaningful percentage of US citizens seem to believe that the government can't be trusted to improve racial equity, there's another nearly equal number who believe government cannot be trusted to foster economic growth. The broad range of issues and the pervasive extent of this trust gap should motivate us to act to rebuild trust in our governing institutions.

What happens when trust is broken? It is the essence of my argument that distrust in the institution of government will have disastrous outcomes. Democratic governments rely on voluntary compliance. It is simply not possible and certainly not desirable to have the government threaten or force citizens into following established norms and rules. Without strong bonds of trust, voluntary compliance suffers. Researchers in the United Kingdom measured what they call the "Cummings Effect,"[10] a significant decline in public confidence in the government's ability to manage COVID-19 as a result of one high-ranking official disregarding lockdown travel restrictions.[11] When trust erodes, the primacy of personal freedoms overtakes rules that are intended to preserve the common good. Heated arguments centering on personal rights pertaining to abortion, gun ownership, even local building codes in the United States all pit what individuals perceive as their rights or best interests against the best interests of our larger society. In turn, the erosion of institutional strength makes the exercise of individual freedoms futile.

Divisiveness is an initial outcome, but from an institutional perspective one of the first areas of government to suffer from eroded trust is its ability to collect revenues. Besley and co-author Torsten Persson introduce their Pillars of Prosperity website[12] with a quote from the eighteenth-century Scottish economist Adam Smith. "Little else is required to carry a state to the highest degree of opulence from the lowest barbarism, but peace, easy taxes, and a tolerable administration of justice; all the rest being brought about by the natural course of things."

In a 2019 report,[13] the OECD (Organisation for Economic Co-operation and Development) indicates that when it comes to taxation not much has changed since Smith's time. OECD refers to what they call "tax morale," or "the intrinsic willingness to pay tax." That would be the "easy taxes" part of Smith's statement.

Since taxes constitute the revenue enabling government to act, reducing its coffers effectively diminishes its resources and capabilities. An underfunded government will necessarily underdeliver on necessary public services. It's easy to see how underdelivery only leads to greater mistrust, less compliance, and increased governmental dysfunction.

Government's Strongest Assets

Just as we looked at the skills and abilities of philanthropy and non-profits, we should consider the unique capacities and resources of democratic governments. More than any of the other foundational forces of philanthropy—nonprofits and corporate—the government distinguishes itself by its access to:

- ◆ Financial resources
- ◆ Human resources
- ◆ Authority
- ◆ Policymaking
- ◆ Scale

FINANCIAL RESOURCES

Through its mandate to tax both individuals and corporations, the federal government can reasonably ensure a predictable, consistent flow of revenue to its coffers. While this money is apportioned across the many branches of government and the budget must be approved by Congressional vote, taxation has proven to be a reliable, "renewable" revenue source. The government is also permitted to operate at a deficit, limited by Congressional approval of appropriations and a weak afterthought agreement on a "debt ceiling."

The Federal Reserve Bank, an independent quasigovernmental organization, is the only entity able to print more currency, set interest rates, and make "monetary policy decisions intended to achieve price stability, full employment, and stable economic growth."[14] The combined power of the government to set both monetary and fiscal policy provides it with exceptional financial resources and capabilities.

HUMAN RESOURCES

According to a 2024 report,[15] the federal government employs approximately three million people, a figure that has remained relatively constant since peaking in 1990, dipping in 2014 to 2.7 million only to rise again to its current level. These millions of employees are engaged in supporting the three branches of government; namely the executive, legislative, and judicial departments or agencies. Spanning a wide range of professional expertise, this workforce represents a massive number of highly skilled workers. Their deep range of education and experience offers an opportunity for multidisciplinary collaboration to address complex issues.

AUTHORITY

The various branches of the federal government have typically represented the highest authority in the United States. The three branches of government, i.e., the executive, legislative, and judicial are intended to form a system of checks and balances to protect against overreach of any one branch, a concept that hopefully makes it past the current administration at the time of this writing. There is no higher authority in the democratic design that can overrule mandates, rules, or regulations set by the federal government, though in a democracy the governed have the right to appeal or protest all decisions by exercising their right to vote.

POLICYMAKING

In matters concerning all aspects of public health and safety, from banking regulations to consumer protection to civil rights, it is the singular responsibility and obligation of the federal government to create and enforce policies for the common good in coordination with state and local governments as well as the industries being regulated.

SCALE

The combination of all of the characteristics cited here, i.e., financial and human resources, ultimate authority, and the ability to set policy, uniquely position the federal government to address complex issues at scale. In his compelling article, Mark Funkhauser[16] cites a Ford

Foundation leader claiming that we have misplaced our hope for social change by relying on the small niche of social entrepreneurs. By way of example, Funkhauser notes that while public education is a $600 billion enterprise, private money garnered from PTA bake sales as well as from huge philanthropic organizations contributes only 1% of the amount required to fund public education. Only government has the ability to scale to the size of the social challenges we face.

Historically the government has funded critical R&D work, leading to commercial breakthroughs in science, medicine, and industry. To return to the example of response to natural disasters, there are demonstrable instances when the extent of need far exceeds the remedies local or private entities can deliver, regardless of extreme generosity or willingness to assist. And the results of our government's R&D efforts have historically been incredible. From the ability to forecast weather, to GPS; from the flu shot to MRIs; from microchips to the internet; and even those ever-present barcodes; none of these would have been brought to bear without the substantial investment by the federal government.

Areas for Engagement

What are examples of some problem areas too big to be left to the private sector? It depends on whom you ask, but here are some voices worth hearing.

Michael Fitzgerald, editor in chief of *Harvard Public Health*, acknowledges that among the jaded, the old putdown "good enough for government work" may still be heard. But Fitzgerald argues, in truth we give our most intractable problems to government to solve. Even hardcore free market champions like Milton Friedman (who Fitzgerald wittily dubs the "Thanos of government-busters") recognize that "We especially want governments to take on things markets don't find profitable enough."[17] Like the aforementioned $600 million behemoth of public education. Fitzgerald's area of concern, not surprising in light of his job, is public health.

He highlights efforts to improve existing public health support the government currently provides as Medicare, Medicaid, and Children's Health Insurance Program (CHIP) that in combination serve about 41% of the US population. Fitzgerald believes we can do even better, beginning with the proposition that we "Think of government as the impetus for addressing social problems at scale." Not as an excuse for why efforts fall short of solutions.

Looking beyond public health, there are many who see opportunities for government investment in infrastructure at scale. In twenty-first century parlance, infrastructure includes more than building out the traditional projects of roads, bridges, and public schools. While the seminal work "Government as a Platform"[18] was written by Tim O'Reilly in 2011, its relevance today and in this context is clear. Encouraging and supporting a shift in the way government officials and workers view their role is critical to realizing the potential government has. Effecting a move away from seeing themselves as a "vending machine emergency service delivery mechanism" to adopting their role as *platform builders and maintainers* is a vital piece of enhancing government impact.

Some innovators within government already see both this need and its opportunities. In January of 2025, Maryland Governor Wes Moore and his CIO stated that Maryland is uniquely situated to take on digital infrastructure, intended to "streamline broadband infrastructure development among state and county entities . . . and help eliminate financial inefficiencies."[19] Their geospatial assets and understanding of property along with the concentration of experts they have working in this space make them eminently qualified to lead this effort that can then be shared across the country. My past experience in state government showed me the tremendous potential savings in time, effort, and dollars such an initiative could produce, along with exponential increases in efficiency. Governments willing and able to create frameworks upon which citizens can co-create services will both drive innovation into government and bring citizens closer to government throughout collaborative efforts.

Another lever that governments uniquely possess is access to troves of data. Much of the data that controls successful policy implementations lives deep inside government databases. When that data is opened up to inform and help shape civic action, solutions can multiply. Data.gov, the federal government's open data site,[20] invites users to access information relevant to their concerns. Sharing what the government knows with those able to lend location or situation specific technical expertise can unlock the power of reliably sourced data.

Instead of useful information stagnating behind shrinking government budgets, it can form the basis for the co-creation of a host of solutions. While the federal government had been moving in past years to open up many of its data stores, much of it is still hidden behind bureaucratic firewalls. Opening up this data and combining it with mountains of state, county, and municipal data could unleash solutions yet to be imagined. Another example of the role that government can play today is to stand in the breach of gaps in the social safety net by acting in collaboration with industry and individuals. Government must make its data leverage accessible to citizens in order to unleash this power. Instead we are seeing alarming signs of reversing this trend toward greater transparency, making data less available to experts across multiple fields such as public health and environmental sciences.

A bit on the wonkier side of government's unique capabilities is its traditional ability to enact rules and regulations. One example might be the establishment of tax shields and tax incentives. This practice involves using taxation or incentives to drive positive behaviors. We've seen some experiments in taxation as leverage in the imposition of tobacco taxes to exert downward pressure on cigarette smoking, or in some municipalities, a hotly contested "soda tax" on sweetened beverages, the proceeds of which fund public schools, libraries, and recreation programs.[21] There is clearly untapped potential for targeted taxes to have a large and direct impact on underfunded segments of society.

On a larger scale, government might apply to the nonprofit sector "tax and trade" systems similar to those that have been rolled out to industry as incentives for environmental actions. Catchafire, the social enterprise where I served as CEO until 2025, worked directly with Impact Genome to create a new system that ultimately could lead to nonprofits being able to utilize a cap and trade approach for social outcomes.[22] With government approval, adoption, and dissemination, our experiment could scale across regions and states, resulting in a sizable increase in impact for many nonprofit organizations and their philanthropic funders. Nonprofits could be able to trade the outcomes they generate directly to individuals and organizations that want to see those outcomes come to life. So, instead of the multiple intermediaries involved with funding our nonprofits, they could directly control their futures with such a system.

An Outcome Orientation

Because many of the services we depend on government to provide are in some respects similar to the work of nonprofits and philanthropies in that their "bottom line" can't be measured in dollars and cents, it's essential that we evaluate these services not simply as activities or outputs, e.g., the number of people served. Having an outcome orientation for government services encourages us to look to what results from these interventions. Often the outcomes can have calculable financial consequences.

Third Sector is a national nonprofit providing technical assistance across government agencies to help reshape their efforts for greater impact. Since its founding in 2011, Third Sector has positioned itself as a partner to government, community-based organizations, and philanthropies and aims to "unlock possibility, confront inequity, and catalyze change to the benefit of the people and places our government, community-based, and philanthropic partners serve."[23] Work that fosters greater collaboration and focuses on measurable outcomes offers a way forward to improve policies, systems, and services across multiple areas of practice on a large scale. And in the process, to rebuild trust in the providers, including the government.

A focus on outcomes can increase our understanding of which public programs and services "work" and which do not. "Outcomes provide a common language with which state and local governments and the nonprofit, private, philanthropic, and academic sectors can communicate their shared and competing visions and expectations of public programs and services. In this capacity, outcomes can spur innovative, multisector partnerships. They can also align program and service implementation with the varying expertise and decision-making preferences and styles of individuals from a multitude of backgrounds."[24]

An outcome orientation, supported by unbiased data, highlights the long-term effectiveness and cost savings associated with more preventative—versus predominantly reactive—social programs and services. Although more preventative programming (for example, prioritizing the education of at-risk youth over more traditional juvenile justice programming) makes financial—not to mention ethical—sense over the long term, state and local governments often cannot

afford the upfront costs required to administer this level of special-
ized service delivery. Preventative programming provides another
instance in which collaboration, in this case involving the commitment of financial resources from philanthropy and private funders
along with government resources, can bridge the gap to significantly
improve service delivery.

The Price of Failure

Your age, occupation, and place of residence would probably help
determine how you would answer this question: what are the most
significant failures of government in the past decade? In his insightful
and sobering 2014 report, Brookings Fellow Paul C. Light lists 41 of
his most notable examples, ranging from the 2001 9/11 terrorist
attacks to a flu vaccine shortage in 2004, a fatal West Virginia mine
collapse in 2006, and in 2013 the Washington Navy Yard shootings,
the Boston Marathon bombing, and the spectacular crash of
HealthCare.gov's newly launched website.[25] National security, public
health, infrastructure, and worker protection, military and civilian
protection, and dependable technology—all failed. And there are
many, in fact too many other instances of catastrophic failures over
this period in our recent history. Light acknowledges that the government has also scored some wins during this time, and that too often
we take for granted ongoing accomplishments like delivering millions of monthly social security checks on time. His intent in this
thoughtful and balanced paper was not to bash government. Instead
his research sought to answer several central questions to enable us
to avoid perpetuating a cascade of failure. Light wants to uncover:
"where did government fail, why did government fail, who caused
the failures, and what can be done to fix the underlying problems?"

Light acknowledges the complex set of people and externalities
that comprise government action and inaction that sets up failure.
"Poorly designed policies come from Congress and the president, for
example, and may be impossible to implement regardless of bureaucratic commitment. Moreover, government cannot always do more
with less, compensate for poor leadership, and manage the confu-
sion created by duplication and overlap on Capitol Hill."

Fast-forward to 2025 and a dramatic power shift in Washington DC. In a US Policy and Regulatory Alert report from December 2024,[26] the authors examine how the rise in executive orders increasingly aim to rescind directives from the previous administration, order agencies to withdraw guidance documents, and issue a rapid flurry of their own new policy mandates. The paper cites the 2024 Supreme Court decision *Loper Bright Enterprises v. Raimondo* that overturned the previously held Chevron doctrine requiring courts to defer to interpretations of ambiguous statutes by the experts within relevant federal agencies. This decision opens the door for more recission most likely aimed at deregulation. The paper's conclusion states, "As the Trump administration enters office, it marks a period of pronounced regulatory uncertainty. The Trump administration itself will likely revisit many of the Biden administration's regulations. Congress may exercise its own power over the regulatory environment, attaching conditions or amendments to continued funding. And the judiciary will see challenges to a host of regulations, both new and old, in the wake of *Loper Bright*." The paper was indeed prescient as the second Trump administration has indeed pushed in each of these directions.

How do we measure the cost of "uncertainty"? Going back to Paul Light's research, we can contrast a government characterized by volatility and uncertainty with the benchmarks Light established for reversing the trend of failure. To be successful in his view, government must have a well-defined, agreed upon vision for success, what I have been referring to as an "outcome orientation." Light states, "Vision with execution is the clear driver of success, just as its absence is an equation for failure." The steps he outlines for improving the government's ability to deliver are clear, measurable, and attainable[27] *if there is a will to set the government up to succeed.*

1. Think about policy effectiveness from the start.
2. Provide the funding, staff, and collateral capacity to succeed.
3. Flatten the chain of command and cut the bloat.
4. Select presidential appointees for their effectiveness, not connections.
5. Sharpen the mission.

An Appetite for Change

It is the essence of my argument in this book that allowing or, worse still, promoting distrust in the institution of government will continue to have disastrous outcomes. For just one example, how can we ignore the panoply of tragic events leading up to and continuing into the pandemic years and the fallout that persists five years later in the form of widespread denial of scientific evidence?

My hope in sharing the data on the erosion of trust in government and the predictable but avoidable outcomes of failure is that this bleak picture should be enough to energize multiple parts of the country. There is supporting evidence to suggest that reform can spring from the grassroots, take hold from the top down, or ideally arise from a combination of both. What would it take? A nonpartisan commitment to the idea that government has a role in advancing the betterment of society for all. And if government is made efficient and transparent in this way, trust in government would start to be rebuilt not by force but by positive effect.

Efforts for reform may begin with a data driven and open public policy reformation of government at all levels. It must include a radical commitment to transparency. It must start with cultivating a deep understanding among Americans of all levels of government, what we used to know as "civics." Voters in a democracy fundamentally need to know what government leaders can do, what they want to do, and where the gaps and overlaps are. We can call for the establishment of a method for collaboration among government officials across levels (i.e., local, state, federal) and across states. Reformation will require people from all sectors across the four forces as well as citizens to press for and engage in repair.

With government forces aligned, our elected officials and career civil servants will be better positioned to enter into collaborations with the other three forces of philanthropy, nonprofits, and corporate entities.

Nobody wants to see the United States as a failed state. Those on the political right believe we are too important to allow this. Those on the left believe the people who will be most negatively impacted are too important to be marginalized. And the large majority in the middle just want to see better outcomes for all. Safety, security, affordable homes, effective education, and the promise of prosperity for their children. A government that lives up to the promise of We the People.

Government and AI

Governments throughout the United States are powerful forces. In terms of helping build stronger communities they provide an incredible amount of resources to multiple social challenges. And as they look to rehabilitate the trust they have lost over the years, now is an opportune time for them to be seen as aiding the most important technological change in centuries. By leveraging their granting powers, governments of all types, the federal, state, and multiple units of local government, can easily lever their granting programs to focus on building strong regional AI centers of excellence based upon the democratization of AI. By making even small grants available to communities looking to work together, local AI solutions stood up in partnership with regional foundations and brought to life with nonprofits' data, can now be connected across the company to have this new technology pointed at creating strong communities rather than just creating new memes for the world to consume. This is one of the major missing pieces as communities struggle to fund programs as well as progress. But government can step up and fill the void and at the same time, rehabilitate their image.

Summary and What's Ahead

In this chapter we discussed the promise and problems with governments in America. We dug deep into the current lack of trust in government Americans have and how that came about. We also now understand why government is so vital to our success and identified where their strongest assets lie. We looked at the incredible hope that we all have in the promise of improving our governments as well as how and where we can engage now. Again, we wrap with how the power of AI can make things better for governments across the board. Next, we will look at some of the same questions and how they apply to corporations in the country.

CHAPTER 5

The Business of Business Is (Not Just) Business

I could be wrong that as part of the money culture of this city and region, not understanding that you have to spend it to make it. And so too often things are done on the cheap and you just wouldn't do it that way if you were in doing it like a business and trying to maximize the moving of metrics . . . For example, the corporate sector who needs consumers and employees should be investing much more in that ecosystem because out of that ecosystem comes both consumers and employees, but that seems to happen at the late end in a reactionary way."
—Walter Lanier, President and CEO,
Great Lakes Urban Empowerment Solutions

By any measure, the US economy is by far the largest, most robust, and powerful in the world.[1]

Capitalism has proven to be a major contributing factor to the growth, wealth, and stability of the United States since declaring its independence from Great Britain in the eighteenth century. It's not surprising that over time the role of business in America has been the subject of discussion, debate, and very divergent opinions. In this chapter we'll explore how our economy has changed over time, some of the resultant twentieth-century attitudes toward business, and how our expectations for acceptable or praiseworthy corporate behavior continue to evolve in the twenty-first century. These shifting beliefs have not only had an impact on how business is conducted but have also had a profound effect on all of us, contributing to our quality of life, our expectations for the future, and our trust in the promise of America.

At the time of this writing in late 2025, the second Trump administration is still unfolding. Many of the current efforts regarding what corporations should, in my view, be focused on are simply the extension of trends found over the past several years. It is very uncertain what the lasting takeaways will be from this administration. The numerous movements unfolding now are too erratic to point to certain conclusions. For our purposes in this book, we will look at the demonstrated trends already in place and will draw conclusions based on existing, stable facts.

Pronouncements from On High

In a 1925 speech to journalists, President Calvin Coolidge expressed his conviction that "After all, the chief business of the American people is business. They are profoundly concerned with producing, buying, selling, investing and prospering in the world."[2] Perhaps today, few would argue that point, although it is a more complex sentiment than the quote that is often misattributed to Coolidge, that "the business of business is business."

By the 1970s, following the Great Depression and two world wars, the American business landscape and the global economy had changed considerably. As if to clarify the aim of American corporations in this new world order, the University of Chicago economist and Nobel laureate Milton Friedman published an influential *New York Times* essay under the headline, "The Social Responsibility of Business Is to Increase its Profits." Simple. Focus on the bottom line. Terms like "shareholder primacy" began to define corporate doctrine. In a short time we experienced seismic changes in American business practices. Hostile takeovers, corporate raiders, junk bonds, the erosion of employee safeguards and benefits packages, all became commonplace methods to improve the bottom line for shareholders. No wonder boardrooms and business schools found it easy to buy into. Profit may be hard to gain but it is relatively easy to measure. Focusing the sector on a single metric was far easier to drive than pursuing a novel, multi-stakeholder analysis measuring a more inclusive definition of corporate success.

"The success of the article was not because (Friedman's) arguments were sound or powerful, but rather because people desperately *wanted* to believe. At the time, private sector firms were starting to feel the first pressures of global competition and executives were looking around for ways to increase their returns. The idea of focusing totally on making money, and forgetting about any concerns for employees, customers or society seemed like a promising avenue worth exploring,. . ."[3]

This drive, largely accelerated by President Reagan's embrace of the single bottom line metric, continued throughout the 1970s, launching subsequent decades of growth often exclusively focused on profitability. Then came the unanticipated financial crisis of 2008 and the call for more accountability in the "free market" where record levels of profit were too often being earned at the expense of people and the planet. What began to emerge was a new paradigm expressed in terms of a corporate commitment to Environmental, Social, and Governance (ESG), namely the environment, social, and governance consequences of business practices. This commitment reached perhaps its highest expression with the issuance of the 2020 Davos Manifesto.[4] Suddenly annual reports included initiatives and impact metrics meant to demonstrate corporate commitment to ESG.

Around this time, Michael Porter, Harvard Professor and legendary business thought leader, started advocating for an approach to business he named "Creating Shared Value" (CSV). He argued that by identifying genuine ways in which a company could stop being "extractive" and instead find ways to create value that mutually supports corporate profits *and* the communities in which companies operate, businesses and society would thrive. When he surveyed the American business landscape, Porter believed public trust in corporate America was badly eroded. Meanwhile nationally and globally, populations faced tremendous environmental, health, and equity challenges that could not be solved by philanthropy or NGOs acting alone. Porter recognized that businesses, unlike nonprofits or governments, are uniquely positioned to create value and generate wealth. Capitalism could be an engine for positive social change.

"Doing well" and "doing good" in his view were not mutually exclusive. In fact CSV practices could provide competitive advantage and sustainable long-term growth for corporations willing to do business differently. He believed CSV "is not corporate social responsibility, philanthropy, or even sustainability, but a new way to achieve economic success."[5]

Impact on the Ground

Over time beliefs originating in academic research or C-suite strategic thinking "trickle down" to become embedded in the way Americans view the role of business. We have seen the general perception of the role of business in society today evolve, reflecting a move away from accepting that corporations should be purely profit-driven focus to a desire for business to adopt a broader, more responsible, and socially conscious approach. In addition to a call for ESG standards, several other movements emerged from the 2008 collapse, namely:

- ◆ Corporate Social Responsibility (CSR)
- ◆ Stakeholder vs. Shareholder Capitalism
- ◆ Workplace and Labor Rights
- ◆ Business Designed as a Force for Change

CORPORATE SOCIAL RESPONSIBILITY (CSR)

As American business seeks a balance between pure profit and corporate caring, it continues to vacillate between the two objectives, viewed by some as mutually exclusive. Businesses are now expected to contribute positively to society, whether through sustainability initiatives, ethical labor practices, community engagement, or philanthropy. Consumers and investors have increasingly favored companies that demonstrate a commitment to social good. While this trend has been solid over the past 10 years, during this past year we have seen a falloff. "Inflows to global sustainable funds plunged $36 billion last year, the lowest since 2018, after ballooning to $645 billion in 2021, shrinking by half while the conventional funds market, driven by US stocks, enjoyed a boom, the analysts said in a note."[6]

STAKEHOLDER CAPITALISM VS. SHAREHOLDER CAPITALISM

The traditional notion that businesses exist solely to maximize shareholder value is being challenged. There is growing advocacy for **stakeholder** capitalism, where companies consider the interests of employees, customers, communities, and the environment alongside financial performance. While in general there has been a shift toward stakeholders, this too has seen backlash over the past few years. So much so that Harvard has published a piece that outlines strategies for management teams interested in stakeholder capitalism to deploy in order to protect support of CSR programs.[7]

WORKPLACE AND LABOR RIGHTS

There is increasing demand for fair wages, better working conditions, and employee well-being. The gig economy, remote work, and automation have raised new questions about job security and worker rights. In the midst of rapid inflation, wage rates have seen pressure as well as a new upsurge in workers interested in labor rights. Public approval of labor unions has reached its highest level in more than half a century. A Gallup poll found that 67% of Americans approved of unions in 2023, with enthusiasm particularly strong among younger workers. A poll commissioned by the AFL-CIO found that 88% of Americans under age 30 have a favorable view of unions.[8]

In light of this, it's perhaps unsurprising that companies who employ young adults, such as Starbucks, REI, Whole Foods, and Amazon have recently been challenged by movements to unionize workers. Though they may be viewed as "progressive" companies, in general their response has been to oppose unionization efforts.

BUSINESS AS A FORCE FOR CHANGE

Many people believe that businesses have the resources and influence to drive meaningful societal progress. In fact, benefit corporations (B-Corps) have been gaining adopters steadily over the past few years. Adopting the benefit corporation structure provides legal protection for mission-driven businesses, allowing directors to consider stakeholders beyond shareholders in decision-making processes. This framework can enhance a company's reputation, attract socially conscious consumers and investors, and ensure mission preservation through leadership changes and capital raises. Patagonia was one of the first examples of a company embracing the benefit corporation structure. The rise of Public Benefit Corporations (PBCs), a subset of benefit corporations, has been notable. These entities are *legally required* to pursue specific public benefits and report transparently on their progress. Companies like Allbirds, Kickstarter, and Warby Parker have adopted the PBC structure to formalize their commitment to social and environmental goals.[9] My experience as CEO of Catchafire, Inc., a certified B-Corp, introduced me to the power of these corporate structures. Far from limiting our choices, these legal obligations enabled me to make decisions that balanced outcomes for *all of our stakeholders*, not just shareholders.

ESG STANDARDS

Companies are judged not only by profitability but also by their ESG performance. Businesses that prioritize sustainability, diversity, ethical governance, and climate action are often viewed more favorably by the public and investors. While the growth of ESG initiatives over the past decade has been incredible, again, the past few years have put that growth in context. Many of the structures put in place to measure ESG efforts have been significant and the most recent outflows from ESG funds appear to be temporary as this market space is entering its mature stage.

ACCELERANTS AND BLOCKERS

The sudden, drastic impact of the COVID-19 global pandemic overturned much of what had come to be considered "business as usual." The widespread shuttering of many businesses, supply chain disruptions, layoffs, and the urgent transition from in person to remote and hybrid work rocked society. Looking back on some of the repercussions, arguably one consequence of the pandemic was a recognition by corporate America of the role they had to play in the overall health and well-being of their employees and their communities. For some businesses that prompted a new or increased commitment to CSR programs and initiatives. One expression of CSR focus resulted in expanding sick leave benefits. Prominent players such as Microsoft, Google, and Twitter made remote work a permanent option for many employees, recognizing work-life balance as an essential part of CSR. Across many industries we saw a rise in employee activism and union organizing, often with gig economy workers demanding more from massive employers such as Amazon and Walmart. Even so-called progressive companies like Starbucks were not immune to activist employees calling for unionization as worker protection.

During this period of social disruption we also saw more acceptance of corporate responsibility for climate change. ESG engagement and adoption of proactive climate protection programs rose dramatically. With huge energy consumers such as Amazon proclaiming their Climate Pledge to be net-zero carbon by 2040, a turning point seemed to be reached. New momentum spurred hundreds of US companies to join a push for climate-friendly policies and practices, despite pandemic-related economic challenges.

The COVID-19 health emergency also revealed the inherent power in public/private partnerships. Two competing large pharma operators, Pfizer and Moderna, played a critical role in vaccine development. In tandem they then acted as trusted partners with the federal and state governments to ensure rapid, equitable, affordable distribution of their vaccines. Corporations had the product expertise and governments had the means to inform, educate, and serve millions of Americans by mobilizing our considerable health care infrastructure for distribution and immunization.

The corporate world's prominent actions supporting social good did not go unnoticed by the general public. Overall public trust in businesses increased during this period, now with even higher expectations for what socially committed business could accomplish. In 2021 the Edelman Trust Barometer[10] placed businesses as the most trusted institution above government and media.

As the pandemic dramatically demonstrated, we live and work in an increasingly hyper-connected world. The globalization of the US economy has meant viewing our business actions abroad through the related lenses of Fair Trade and environmental impact. Fair Trade demands originally led to pressure to increase labor standards globally. These expectations for fair labor practices have driven us to demand that sourcing simply be returned to the United States where employee protections and regulations are already in place. Meanwhile corporations looking to operate multinationally are compelled to comply with complex and varied global standards. The new Trump administration is pushing hard on this dynamic. Only time will tell in a few years if the capitalists agree with this direction.

According to a study by the World Economic Forum[11] "there is also a shift in corporate ESG disclosures, which are moving from voluntary to mandatory, with new government regulations coming fast."

On the domestic front, recently American society and the US corporate world have been rocked by events that have prompted swift, significant reevaluations of our identity and actions as a democracy. Business has not been exempted from feeling the repercussions of the collision of two opposing shifts in the values and beliefs of Americans.

First came an accelerant to social equity issues in 2020 as a result of public outcry over the George Floyd murder. "The 2020 mass protests in response to the deaths of George Floyd and Breonna Taylor had a significant impact on American corporations. Several large public companies pledged an estimated $50 billion to advancing racial equity and committed to various initiatives to internally improve diversity, equity, and inclusion."[12]

A mere four years later, as if operating like a social law of thermodynamics that for every progressive push for social equity there is an equal, opposite reaction, we are witnessing sweeping withdrawals expressed as radical anti-DEI backlash of 2024–2025. This Forbes article[13] is a good, yet depressing, summary of corporations that have already capitulated to the efforts of the Trump administration to roll back any and all perceived DEI programs. This same piece includes mention of those brave souls that have taken a stand in favor of diversity efforts, namely Delta, Costco, Deutsche Bank, Apple, Cisco, JPMC, and NASDAQ.

Where this push and pull over the expression of our democratic principles lands is as yet unknown. Most likely, though, corporations will be important players. Anyone interested in pushing our communities forward will most decisively want to include and engage American corporations in the solutions they develop.

A Very Brief History of American Industry

The extraordinary rise of the American economy over the past 250 years is not without its implications for shaping our values and beliefs as a nation. Quite rapidly we have moved from an agrarian to an industrialized economy, then we underwent offshoring and transitioned to a largely service economy. While services are still a substantial component of our GDP (Gross Domestic Product), the dizzying advance of technology pushes our economy toward one characterized by knowledge work. Each of these stages of economic upheaval, what we also consider "progress," has left its mark on the workforce. In this section let's look briefly at some of the implications these changes in the nature of work have had on our values, beliefs, and priorities.

AGRICULTURAL TO INDUSTRIAL ECONOMY (PRE-1900s–MID-1900s)

These were the main events of the industrial economy:

- ◆ *Workforce Homogeneity*

    In an agricultural society, work was largely local, family-based, and homogenous, limiting the demand for workplace diversity initiatives. While there were regional differences based on climate, available natural resources, and access to markets, farmers and producers were more likely to share similar ambitions, expectations, and as land owners, to make long-term investments in their community.

- ◆ *Industrialization and Labor Movements*

    As the economy shifted to industrialization, mass migration and urbanization brought together diverse labor forces and created new tensions. The massive migration of millions of Blacks out of the rural south to industrialized northern cities changed neighborhoods and the labor force considerably. Despite the claims for equality of rights and opportunities made by many northerners, workplace segregation and discrimination were widespread.[14]

- ◆ *Union Influence*

    Labor unions in the early twentieth century were initially exclusionary, designed to protect the existing interests of one narrowly defined group, often by country of origin or trade, against "newcomers" or competitors. Over time unions came to play a larger role by advocating for broad worker protections across industries and, indirectly, for greater workforce inclusion.[15]

Unions came to be the main method workers had to achieve any balance of power in negotiations with employers and to affect policy changes such as the length of the workday to ensure worker rights for safe and fair working conditions.

INDUSTRIAL TO SERVICE ECONOMY (MID-1900s–LATE 1900s)

These were the main events of the service economy:

- *Civil Rights Era and Affirmative Action*

  As the United States transitioned from manufacturing to a service-based economy, federal policies (e.g., Civil Rights Act of 1964, affirmative action) forced companies to adopt more inclusive hiring practices.[16] In addition to the changes these laws brought to the political realm, economic historians highlight the economic gains resulting from both the Civil Rights Act and The Voting Rights Act.

- *Corporate Diversity Programs Begin*

  The rise of large service-oriented industries such as finance, retail, and health care led to increased customer interactions across new swaths of American consumers. As companies sought to expand their customer acquisition, recruiting a more diverse workforce proved valuable in reaching and serving a newly diverse consumer base.[17]

- *Backlash Begins*

  Some conservative critics began viewing affirmative action and early DEI programs as forced compliance rather than merit-based hiring and admissions, laying the groundwork for future opposition.[18] Pushback to these programs has had serious implications for higher education as well as corporations, especially at the C-suite and board level.

SERVICE TO KNOWLEDGE ECONOMY (1990s–PRESENT)

These were the main events of the knowledge economy, thus far:

- *Globalization and Tech Boom*

  The knowledge economy, led by technology, finance, and health care, placed an emphasis on innovation, cognitive skills, and digital transformation. Many DEI initiatives expanded during this time as companies saw diverse teams as beneficial for creativity and global reach.[19]

◆ *DEI Expansion in Corporate America*

Major corporations launched formal diversity and inclusion initiatives, driven by consumer expectations, investor pressure, and evidence suggesting that diverse teams improve business performance.[20]

◆ *Rising Resistance*

As the knowledge economy grew, highly skilled workers, often in STEM (science, technology, engineering, and mathematics) fields, started questioning race- and gender-based hiring preferences, seeing them as potentially disadvantaging their meritocracy. The political polarization around identity-based policies intensified. Much of this resistance started with a Google action here.[21]

ANTI-DEI SENTIMENT IN THE KNOWLEDGE ECONOMY (2020s)

These were the main events of the current anti-DEI sentiment:

◆ *Tech Industry and Economic Shifts*

Many tech and finance firms that once championed DEI are now rolling back these efforts. Some argue that in a highly competitive, AI-driven economy, merit-based hiring should take precedence over diversity.[22] Others analyze the error in thinking that AI is without embedded bias, warning that relying on AI to impose fairness is misguided. New research signals that AI simply makes the discrimination of the past more efficient.

◆ *Legal and Political Shifts*

The 2023 Supreme Court decision striking down affirmative action in college admissions reinforced broader skepticism toward DEI programs, accelerating many corporate cutbacks. This is just a partial listing of the legal challenges with potentially devastating impact on access and opportunity: *Students for Fair Admissions, Inc. v. President and Fellows of Harvard College* and *Students for Fair Admissions, Inc. v. University of North Carolina.*

◆ *Economic Pressures*

In times of economic downturn such as those recently experienced during post-pandemic layoffs and even more recent tech industry slowdowns, DEI roles are among the first to be eliminated. The general perception is that these programs do not generate revenue. The development of Inclusive Economics, a concept advocating for "integrating diversity into the core of our economic systems" for sound business reason, directly challenges the alleged financial downsides of DEI.[23]

◆ *Rise of "Anti-Woke" Sentiment*

Some corporations face backlash from investors and consumers who see DEI as unnecessary or politically driven, leading to policy reversals.[24] Many of these corporate changes have been in response to their consumer base in conservative or rural market segments. Companies like John Deere and Anheuser-Busch that have rolled back DEI initiatives largely sell to a rural demographic that aligns to the conservative political efforts in this space.

Who Our Heroes Are Matters

Just as we witness swings in public opinion, policy direction, and corporate practice, we have seen business leaders rise and fall in our estimation. Who we admire and praise as business leaders reveals our estimation of what the corporate world can and should do.[25] Given the complexity and enormity of the organizations they lead, no leader can be reduced to a few key traits. And just as changes in the market may prompt leaders to pivot their organizations, responding to social and political changes may cause prominent leaders to change course.

Here we look at four leaders who have recently achieved prominence for their visionary leadership and tremendous success.

TIM COOK

Tim Cook, CEO of Apple, is noted for his leadership in maintaining Apple's dominant global market position and its firm commitment to ensuring user privacy and environmental sustainability. Some of the measures enacted under his tenure include:

- **Environmental Commitments:** Apple aims to be carbon neutral across its supply chain by 2030, with significant investments in renewable energy and sustainable materials.
- **Diversity and Inclusion:** Cook has publicly advocated for LGBTQ+ rights and workplace diversity.
- **Privacy and Ethics:** He has positioned Apple as a leader in user data protection, emphasizing privacy as a fundamental right.

Cook recently showed up as an enabler to the Trump administration as well as the Chinese government, agreeing to invest billions to build an Apple facility in Texas. While much of Apple manufacturing is still located in China, it will be instructive to see how Apple responds to the pressure of the new Trump administration to relocate significant amounts of manufacturing to the United States. To date Apple has not signaled a focus on manufacturing and labor standards that reflect American worker priorities. Rather than moving to create domestic manufacturing, they appear to be shifting production centers from China to India.

MARY BARRA

Mary Barra, CEO of General Motors, is acknowledged for steering the company toward electric vehicles and fostering diversity in the traditionally conservative automotive industry. Her notable accomplishments, in addition to rising to the C-suite in a traditionally male-dominated industry, include:

- **Sustainability Leadership:** GM is investing heavily in electric vehicles (EVs) and has pledged to eliminate tailpipe emissions from light-duty vehicles by 2035.
- **Workforce Development:** Barra has championed gender equality and STEM education, particularly for women in the automotive industry.
- **Community Engagement:** GM contributes to disaster relief efforts and supports workforce training programs.

Barra has yet to openly oppose a global trade war built on punitive tariffs. It is unclear how Barra will respond to directives from the new Trump administration to move manufacturing from their NAFTA/USMCA-designed North American footprint to a new, capital-intensive relocation to the union-dominated industry in the United States.

SATYA NADELLA

Satya Nadella, CEO of Microsoft, is credited with revitalizing the company through cloud computing and by embracing a "growth mindset" culture. He has also embraced an HR methodology that highlights layoffs of long-term employees.[26] Signal achievements include:

- ◆ **AI for Good:** Microsoft runs initiatives to use AI for accessibility, health care, and climate action.
- ◆ **Carbon Commitment:** Microsoft has pledged to become carbon negative by 2030, meaning it will remove more carbon than it emits.
- ◆ **Philanthropy:** Under Nadella, Microsoft has increased investments in digital literacy, affordable internet access, and racial justice initiatives. He has also widely opened up support of Microsoft staff priorities spurring a dramatic increase in scope and amount of corporate donations.

JENSEN HUANG

Jensen Huang, CEO of Nvidia, is recognized for his role in rapidly advancing AI technology and graphics processing.

- ◆ **AI and Education:** Nvidia supports AI research in medicine, sustainability, and education.
- ◆ **Environmental Initiatives:** Nvidia designs energy-efficient GPUs, contributing to sustainable computing.
- ◆ **Diversity and Inclusion:** Huang promotes AI education for underserved communities, particularly in STEM fields.

In an increasingly competitive market as China enters the race for AI dominance, his next moves will be closely watched to see how Nvidia acts to retain market share and profitability.

Fallen Heroes

Reaching the pinnacle of business success and fame is no guarantee of future admiration.

Not that long ago we witnessed what was nearly an unthinkable fall from grace as Enron, famously self-regarded as a behemoth run by "the smartest guys in the room"[27] was revealed in 2001 to be an elaborate accounting scam.[28] The collapse of Enron took down the venerable accounting firm Arthur Andersen and shook confidence in what had seemed to be institutions of unimpeachable integrity.

Emerging businesses, especially in what are seen as innovative markets, can rocket to prominence by attracting huge investments and lots of media attention. Theranos, founded and led by Elizabeth Holmes (who imitated Steve Jobs), plummeted in four years from a valuation of $9 billion to bankruptcy and for Holmes a criminal conviction and prison sentence for fraud.[29]

Next came Sam Bankman-Fried, a much-touted champion of cryptocurrency. His FTX empire unraveled at a breathtaking rate, resulting in the loss to investors of millions of dollars and to conviction and imprisonment for Bankman-Fried. Crypto investing attracted legions of young investors, drawn by Bankman-Fried's youthful appeal and counterculture style. Perhaps because of the number of small investors who were taken in, the public response to the FTX scandal was marked by a loss of confidence in cryptocurrency platforms, demands for stricter regulatory oversight, and a broader skepticism regarding the stability and integrity of the crypto industry.

The media covered the rise and fall of FTX extensively but the caution many investors seemed to adopt in the aftermath of its collapse seems to have waned. Crypto is again on the rise.[30]

Much has been written about the speed of the news cycle and the brevity of our contemporary, hyper-wired attention spans. There are other examples than the crypto market with similar outcomes moving quickly from outrage to indifference or even dismissal. Intense media attention can stimulate in the public sector an obsession with the details and perhaps a cry for reform or retribution. When the outrage or indignation dies down, to be replaced by the next trending topic, so does the public concern and any efforts at avoiding a repeat criminal performance.

In a fascinating study of a phenomenon they call "target pressure," researchers Tom Reider and Alex Gillespie investigated the causes of some of these scandals.[31] They define target pressure as "an organizational culture of pressurizing employees to achieve unrealistic goals." Their investigation finds target pressure culture to be the general cause of most of these corporate scandals of inflated achievement and unsubstantiated claims for results or returns on investment. Target pressure culture is created by entrepreneurs and rising senior executives at least in part as their response as aspiring business leaders to earn the respect bestowed on high achievers. Becoming obsessed with rapid growth and rewarding it with huge financial windfalls of investment and valuation often leads to shockingly immoral scandals and spectacular falls from grace.

Public attention is short-lived and the appetite for regulation often disappears with the fading headlines. In other words, these shams and scams are likely to continue, especially if we as consumers do not push back against allowing corporations the license to do whatever it takes to deliver an ever-fattening bottom line for their investors.

Winners and Losers

Given all the attention routinely devoted to tracking activity on Wall Street, one might come to believe that the stock market is synonymous with the US economy. A recent survey revealed that 87% of households with income more than $100,000 have some investment in the stock market, while only 25% of households with incomes less than $40,000 are investors. It's safe to assume that wealthy individuals tend to have larger portfolios than lower-income investors, suggesting that the real distribution of stock market gains disproportionately accrues to the top tier earners.

So who benefits from corporations striving to meet investor expectations for ever higher returns? It's a short list:

+ Investors
+ CEOs, board members, and senior executives who own equity
+ Large corporations and category leaders
+ Customers who may gain short-term pricing advantages
+ Economies with high business activity

Potentially on the losing side are less visible, less vocal groups such as:

- **Employees:** Pressured to increase productivity, may face low wages, long hours, or layoffs in cost-cutting efforts
- **Small businesses:** May struggle against large corporations with profit-driven competitive advantages
- **Consumers (long-term):** May experience lower quality products or monopolistic price hikes as competitors are eliminated
- **Environment and Society:** Businesses focused on short-term profits may neglect sustainability and ethical responsibilities, contributing to pollutants, climate change, and community health risks

The Unique Capabilities of Business

My intention in this chapter is certainly not to bash or blame large corporations for all the ills of the environment and society. What I would like to do is spotlight the tremendous power corporations hold and suggest how those strengths can be directed to result in far more than just fabulous wealth for a small segment of the population.

Unlike the other "forces" we've described, namely, nonprofits, philanthropy, and government, corporations possess certain strengths that they are able to bring to bear in ways that contribute to their longevity and influence. Specifically, corporations are well positioned to:

- Create value by meeting (or driving) the demand for goods and services
- Identify renewable sources of revenue by opening or expanding markets
- Invest in R&D to drive innovation
- Scale their operations to increase productivity and profitability
- Influence markets
- Build wealth for investors *and* stakeholders
- Align their corporate goals with their community goals

We admire businesses that are innovators and value creators, those entities that find ways to make our lives more comfortable and convenient. Interestingly, some recent polls suggest we want these same companies to accept more responsibility by acting in ways that benefit more of the population by addressing concerns that go beyond mere comfort and convenience.

For example, 55% of Americans, according to a 2023 Pew research report,[32] think that the energy industry can do a lot to reduce the effects of climate change and 52% say this about other large businesses and corporations outside of the energy industry. In essence, more than half of those polled urge corporations to address climate change in their operations. Far fewer (27%) respondents felt that individual Americans can do a lot to reduce climate impacts; we need the scale and commitment of the corporate world to bring about meaningful change.

If we look beyond the specifics of energy use and climate change, other recent studies indicate the consumer thinks companies can do more to improve everyday quality of life. 81% of Americans want companies to operate in ways that improve consumers' lives.[33] And according to a 2022 Edelman Trust Barometer,[34] 60% of Americans expect CEOs to take a stand on social issues they deem important such as economic inequality, racial justice, and health care access.

Corporations and AI

Corporations throughout the world hold many unique assets. In my career I have become familiar with many of them, but none quite as deeply as my time at Digital Realty Trust working for the world's leader in building and operating datacenters. These insights brought to light an interesting current dichotomy that can be leveraged into helping build strong communities.

Companies have gone through quite a transformation from when they first started leveraging technology. From server rooms, to carrier's data floors, to their own datacenters, companies have always been on the cutting edge of tech. But they have also owned trailing edge technology for decades after they needed it, leading to waste and inefficiency, but unavoidably so, due to long term commitments demanded by technology and real estate providers. But now, that dichotomy could help us all build stronger communities.

With the onset of the new AI frontiers I have discussed so far in this book, companies have a potentially very large role to play. The new world of corporate computing consists of an ever deepening commitment to high density compute. This includes some of the GPU focused high density requirements of traditional AI. This leaves corporations with an ever depreciating asset of lower density data-center space that their IT teams are always trying to transition from. These assets, however, perfectly fit the mold of the new affordable, secure, and scalable AI discussed earlier in the book. So now, corporates are in the unique position of being able to make their depreciating assets available to the community in need of the same, to develop a new coordinated artificial intelligence targeted at building strong communities sitting inside of their lower density datacenters. We all have roles to play in this brave new world and corporations are no different.

Summary and What's Ahead

When confronted by changes in markets and shifts in consumer sentiment or priorities, it falls to the boards of directors, the CEOs, and the C-suite team to set the corporate direction. With shifting political winds, especially as new policies or executive orders affect immigration, DEI initiatives, and federal regulatory oversight, corporate leaders face decisions with far-reaching implications for society well beyond their shareholders or consumer base. Corporations have always been important, but now they seem to be critical, decisive decision-makers in a battle that could strengthen America again.

However, despite evidence supporting the belief that "doing good and doing well" are not mutually exclusive, corporations may choose to step back from their commitment to ESG, DEI, and other "progressive" practices. The risks to society are great. A failure to act on climate change, increasing profits that accelerate an already unprecedented wealth gap, a return to systemic discrimination by touting "meritocracy," will all contribute to exacerbating some of the divisive issues of our time.

Each of the other society shaping forces of government, philanthropy, and nonprofits lack both the financial resources and the expertise corporations possess. If we are to make meaningful change in addressing society's underlying inequities, none of these forces alone come close to matching the power inherent in collaboration.

In the next chapter, we'll look at each of the four forces through the lens of "radical rebuilding." It's time to consider what each entity may do *independently* to improve their impact, regain trust, and bolster their standing in society. Despite the very different nature of each of these forces, there are commonalities for areas of improvement worth identifying. If each force commits to rethinking aspects of their structure and operation, they may then be better positioned to leverage their individual resources to become truly transformative agents for positive social impact.

PART 2

The Solution: The Perseverance Playbook

CHAPTER 6

Radical Rebuilding with Perseverance Groups

"Equity is an engine, a decision-making engine, an analysis engine that allows you to achieve your mission, to serve, and to create change faster and more efficiently. It is not a buzzword, and it is not a T-shirt, and it is not a random illegal threat. It is a responsibility and a tool to identify who you want to impact. Let's look at who is most harmed and let's put them in the center, and then let's actually build around them. Because we know that if we center those who are most harmed by any sort of policy or need, and we make sure that they are okay, and that we change our policies and systems to accommodate them, the echo effect of so many people who are helped is everyone. Everyone benefits from that."

**—Angelique Power, President and CEO,
Skillman Foundation**

During his senior year at Boston College, Tip O'Neill ran for a seat on the Cambridge City Council. He lost, but this proved to be his only election defeat in a lifetime of public office. What is noteworthy about his failed bid in 1935 was the insight that became his most enduring quote, "All politics is local."[1]

O'Neill, who later went on to be the powerful Democratic Speaker of the House from 1977 to 1987, believed that politicians succeed when they understand and respond to the ordinary, simple concerns of their constituency. Winning elections is not about running on abstractions, ideologies, or grand visions. Voters generally elect those who promise to address the personal issues that most affect their daily lives. Governing is about delivering on those promises.

Throughout the previous chapters, I've explored the past and current states of the four forces of society: nonprofits, philanthropy, government, and business. In this and the following chapters, I'll be making a case for how each of these institutions needs to change if we are to restore and support a more equitable life for all. My argument builds on O'Neill's belief with a twist: while all politics is local, organizing must occur first.

It is becoming clear the federal government is no longer a reliable source for addressing our day-to-day concerns. As we witness a radical pendulum swing away from government interventions at the national level toward decentralization and downsizing, we're about to feel the hurt of not having that Big Brother to help us. We are seeing the politicization of the court system, leading many to question if US courts can deliver the justice that they seek. Businesses are rapidly backing away from previous pledges to progressive goals around climate, equity, and social responsibility. As a recent *New York Times* report showed, from 2024 to 2025 mention of DEI initiatives in particular dropped by nearly 60% across nearly every sector of the US economy.[2]

Nonprofits and philanthropy can't close all the gaps left by government and business in retreat. All four forces must work in concert.

The direction of contemporary civil society, which some may describe as a downward spiral, may appear very depressing, distressing, or even hopeless. But this is where the labor activist in me comes to life. I propose a radically different approach to rebuilding our broken systems by starting at the foundation and then by beginning to find solutions where you live and work, not reflexively looking to Washington DC to solve our problems.

Community and Communication as Bedrock

It all starts here, coming back to the realization that all politics—in fact, most everything that matters—is present at the local level. Building community through communication is the most effective way to rebuild our environment in ways that speak to our commonly held values.

My lived experience has convinced me that institutions, not just individuals, have the potential for the greatest impact. When as an institutionalist I view the current state of the most visible institutions in each of the four areas of nonprofits, philanthropy, government, and business, it's apparent that they all need to be strengthened. One critical area lacking in each of these arenas is trust. As previously cited in Chapter 1, public trust in nearly every one of these four forces is badly eroded. The thing about trust is that it cannot be mandated. It must be earned. There are no shortcuts to restoring trust because durable trust is the hard-won result of real needs being heard, solutions being proposed, actions coordinated and agreed upon, and most importantly, measurable results being delivered. No excuses, no fake reports, no gridlock, no vast amounts of money spent with no return on investment. As a population we are looking for things to change, even when the problems we identify are huge and seemingly intractable like poverty or hunger. So where do we begin?

Convening is a Superpower

There's an old film starring Harrison Ford that is set in a Pennsylvania community of Amish farmers. One of the film's lovely set pieces captures a day of communal barn building. The landowner farmer has picked the barn site and set the date. At dawn literally everyone of all ages turns up bringing to the project whatever resources they have: tools, materials, skills, expertise, muscle, food, and a commitment to the cooperative process. What would have been literally impossible for the farmer to do on his own happens seamlessly on a long, sweaty day. The result is a beautifully framed barn the farmer will now be able to finish as he chooses, completed to suit his specific farming needs. Delivered through cooperative coordination.

That's the Hollywood version, but it isn't impossible to imagine American neighbors pulling together to help each other in times of need. Historically Americans have been generous in responsive to calamity and disasters. We saw this on a national scale after 9/11 and again across the country during COVID-19, though admittedly there was more pushback and friction from dissenting voices in 2020 than we experienced after the September 11 attacks in 2001. No organization or institution issued a proclamation that we should look to our communities to see what could be done. As a society we have found ways to engage and assist. Imagine how much more impact our willingness to make a difference would be if we had the resources and organizing abilities, plus the coordination of our major institutions supporting and guiding us.

The first step in the radical rebuilding process I propose is for leaders from the four institutional forces of nonprofits, philanthropy, government, and business to sit down together, face to face, on a local level. Their task would be clear but not simple: to conduct an honest needs, strengths, and gaps assessment of their community's well-being. Without bias or self-protection, using their deep connections to the individuals they serve, these entities could create a map of the relative strengths and weaknesses within their region. What are the issues their community feels are most pressing? Who among them are underserved? What work is under-resourced? Where are efforts duplicative? Where are innovative service providers struggling to find a foothold? What resources can be shared? What entities and efforts can be combined, eliminated, or stood up to provide a more effective way forward?

I propose we call these efforts "Perseverance" plus the specific city name. "Perseverance" because what we intend to do through these convenings is to build strong communities that stand the test of time. Using the city name allows the efforts to be driven locally, even if our power aggregates nationally. So, in Milwaukee, for instance, we would call these convenings "Perseverance Milwaukee."

If these four forces worked in close collaboration with their constituents and with each other, communities could build up new institutions around their most pressing needs. Necessary public services would be designed and delivered through the conversations these conveners were having with and in the community, replacing the top-down and go-it-alone approach we mostly have now. This approach enables building a base of support and a plan of action from common bonds and agreements. There are examples in our past, historically the labor union movement and more recently the political movement "Indivisible," that show how a national movement can be constructed from many local efforts. The result can be a resilient and responsive infrastructure of local Perseverance Councils that become regional, and eventually national centers for organized, coordinated action. These will begin as loose aggregations, with no taxation, and no official mandate but with the discipline to hold regular meetings locally, then quarterly in regions, and annually as national power centers.

We need to encourage this process of creating hyper-local affinity groups if you will, to build new, larger, and more enduring social bonds to create the future we need to survive. Convening efforts should begin at the city and regional levels and be ongoing, providing community leaders, nonprofits, elected officials, and business executives with the opportunity to get together and get to know each other again, or in many instances get acquainted for the first time. Building up trusted Perseverance Councils will create empowered local communities greater than any one force in an area, over time generating stability and growing trust.

The convener's role is one of neutrality because only a nonpartisan approach will empower these disparate, often competing groups to tackle hard questions honestly and impartially. Each participating institution and organization will need to own up to a true measure of their capacity. That means being frank about where their gaps are along with where their strengths lie.

Once each entity has put their cards on the table, as it were, the valuable mapping process can commence by addressing the following six questions:

1. **Strengths:** What resources and assets do we have as a group?
2. **Duplication:** Are there areas or concerns receiving too much emphasis?
3. **Disinvestment:** Is there work that no longer needs to be done or can at least become a lower priority?

4. **Corporate Allies:** What companies are trying to do the right thing for our community?
5. **Governmental Gaps:** What government programs are strong? Which are floundering?
6. **Prioritized Shifts:** How can we redistribute our collective assets and resources to improve our chances of success?

Armed with these insights, communities will be empowered to stand up the institutional efforts necessary to deal with their local needs themselves. Are there bound to be conflicts and tensions? Guaranteed. But with mature leadership such groups can learn to deal with them openly and resolve stalemates in a meaningful way. If we stay focused on the main goal that allows us to stop replicating efforts and unleash our power as collaborators, such groups are much more likely to be able to point to shared wins for their communities. It doesn't take massive amounts of capital to get started. That first convening session can be as simple as breaking bread together on a First Friday.

Laying the Groundwork

In the previous chapters we've looked at the unique strengths and shortcomings of each of the four institutional forces. Preparatory to engaging in the sort of coalition building we're describing in this chapter, each of the four forces has some prework to do.

NONPROFITS

For nonprofits, making the mindset change away from describing activities to quantifying impact is essential. Impact Genome[3] is showing the way for nonprofits to begin to think of themselves as change agents making a quantifiable difference in their communities. This means moving from ticking off numbers of client contacts, for example, to embracing and measuring outcomes-based action. Nonprofits should be redefining themselves in terms of ROI for donated dollars; e.g., each dollar donated provides two nutritious hot meals or each dollar invested closes the wealth gap in our city by $500 annually. This orientation will also allow for much more insightful investment in social outcomes from areas of capital that want to do good work.

PHILANTHROPY

Philanthropy will be a much more powerful contributor to convenings if they can adopt a mindset that allows for more nimble responses to changing needs. As a recent example of the limitations arising from conventional thinking, after the George Floyd murder and the emergence of the Black Lives Matter movement in 2020 it was challenging to get endowments to make racial equity commitments. Their traditional response was a tendency to defend whatever their foundation had historically funded. There was no room or little appetite for change. In addition, demonstrating a willingness to move the needle beyond a 4–5% annual level of giving on an as-needed basis would make a huge difference in filling a short-term capital needs gap. Moreover, unleashing the power of leverage based on endowments would expand even further the financial impact philanthropy can attain. On the investment side, philanthropy could be increasing their impact by entering into agreements with benefit corporations aligned with their values and goals. This is a largely untapped opportunity for foundations to form strong alliances with corporations to advance shared goals, something community foundations should be pursuing as well. And as we are beginning to see with several innovative philanthropists, participating more fully in trust-based philanthropy is reaping benefits for funders, nonprofits, and their served communities.

GOVERNMENT

We are already seeing dramatic changes in the seat of government power. As more resources and obligations fall to the states, we have an opportunity and a responsibility to shift our focus away from the federal level to the local, state, and regional levels. Governments at every level have the unique ability to make change happen. Re-engaging local citizens in their institutions such as school boards and zoning boards, tax commissions, and parks and recreation initiatives will have an appreciable impact. One major contribution governments at all levels can make is the free and fair dissemination of the massive amounts of data they collect and manage. By making their data available to all people in a way that is rational and true, government can become a platform for developed solutions based on fact. With access to reliable data, nonprofit, philanthropic, and business partners can be far more successful in co-creating services with government officials to meet local needs. When our government at all levels opens their data to community and invites the now more informed community to respond with ideas, engagement, and involvement, the likelihood of success increases. Opening up data across many areas could help inform solutions for critical housing needs, job training and development, and investment in other areas of great value to the community.

CORPORATES

There's a relatively simple, already proven step that corporations could take to increase their positive societal impact: release the C-suite's stranglehold on charitable giving and open it up to all employees. We have already seen large enterprises such as Microsoft experience a significant uptick in giving when employees were given the opportunity to contribute to issues of importance to them, not only to the personal projects of the senior executive team. Encouraging employees to give not only of their money but of their time and expertise contributes to the tremendous value of volunteering that strengthens and helps professionalize the nonprofit sector. Unlocking the latent power of skills-based volunteering that lives inside every American corporation would unleash unbelievable levels of socially aware productivity.

Who Lights the Fuse?

There's no single formulaic approach for how to kickstart the virtuous cycle of convening, but there are some prerequisites. This takes us back to where we started this chapter, and the premium placed on trust. Whoever makes the first move offers the first round of invitations, and volunteers to get the conversation started has to be at least somewhat known and definitely trusted. While it may seem counterintuitive in this time of political divisiveness, this role may be taken up by a local political leader who is interested in moving things forward and has a reputation for being a "doer." Their level within the government might be anything from mayors to county executives, supervisors, or council people. They have the advantage of being known locally by the population and have more visibility, perhaps, than leaders from nonprofits, philanthropies, or businesses.

In some regions it's possible that foundations, perhaps especially community foundations, may be able to get things started as conveners, especially in urban areas where they tend to have more presence. Just as the needs and resources vary greatly by geography and culture, so will the profile of the ideal convener. There are some general criteria that can help identify which entity may be best suited for the role in any region. These traits and resources are essential to increase the likelihood of success by an initial convener:

◆ Be recognized as a broad-based connector
◆ Have credibility in their community
◆ Be viewed as largely independent (not a political agent)
◆ Operate collaboratively
◆ Have certain physical assets such as a convenient and accessible building
◆ Be frustrated with the current state of affairs and believe change is possible
◆ Show a bias toward taking positive action

Successful organizations such as the United Way have shown us the value of handing off leadership smoothly over time. The United Way has regular transitions of their local leadership despite having a national presence. The local leaders come from multiple sources, including business leaders who often serve for a period and then pass the torch to someone else. Whoever takes the lead in launching a convening should build such transitions into the plan. The first year takes a strong founder, but one who is not wedded to the perpetual wielding of control. The more power is reliably and predictably shared over time among the entities, the greater the bond of trust and sense of accountability and responsibility accrues to the group. What ties the conveners and the convened together is a clear, enduring commitment to serving as change agents for an evolving, responsive, and holistic community purpose and the good of society.

I have started an effort to publish a simple Perseverance Handbook as a guidebook to help local groups get started. This handbook is intended as an idea generator, encouraging each local group to adapt it to their own needs. Its main value is in giving everyone a place to start, which is often the hardest part.

Perseverance and AI

When all four forces are convened as anticipated by this chapter, the data created will be massive. And if we don't pay attention to it specifically, the value of it all may not be realized. But if we use Perseverance Councils as a way to coordinate the building of community AI, we can point the power of this technology to the outcomes needed to build strong communities. The details of how this will play out will certainly fill multiple books, but I hope that we have spelled out what each of the four forces must do to make this vision a reality. And I hope that we have kept each force's burden relatively low to allow for incredible performance in this space. I anticipate that the Perseverance Councils will have as one of their most important outcomes the creation of this type of joined system; which will benefit strong communities.

Summary and What's Ahead

In this chapter we started by understanding the true power in communities and the importance of communication among them. We then discussed the power of convening that some of us have in our communities. Importantly we reviewed the detailed work that must be done by each of the four forces as your specific community prepares on their perseverance journey. And we gave some details on what you should be looking for in leaders in your effort. In the next chapter we will get down into the details of how to make all this effort work.

CHAPTER 7

Creating a Perseverance Group

"There isn't a quick fix and a quick solution. There is sort of intentional, steady, repeated progress and work toward a goal. And, you know, when you are just getting in that space, that can feel really unfulfilling. . .You have to find the small wins where you can find them and acknowledge the process along the way."

—Nadege Souvenir, CEO,
San Antonio Area Foundation

In the preceding chapters I hope I've laid out a convincing argument that the time is now for systemic change, and that it's critical to understand that effective change will be achieved only when all four forces of our society commit to transforming how they operate, cooperate, and collaborate.

Fortunately, there are some innovative organizations whose success provides hope and guidance. Drawing on my own experience in addition to studying the playbook for relatively recently established models such as Indivisible, in this chapter I propose a handbook for local leaders who are motivated to drive change in their own communities. Because real change is rooted in identifying regional needs and resources, this proposed framework is designed to leave space for customization. In fact, local efforts to unify the four forces operating in a specific area have to begin by deeply under-standing local conditions and priorities. While these will most likely vary region to region, there are foundational principles that will help leaders anywhere stand up a new, more broadly based and sup-ported coalition for fixing their broken systems.

It will certainly benefit most nonprofits and other coalition mem-bers to address each of these four pillars of:

1. Maturity Modeling
2. Coalition Building
3. Governance
4. Outcome Orientation

However, before any philanthropic, corporate, or governmental teams, divisions, or departments leap into the creation of a larger, cross-sector entity, **completing a maturity model assessment will strengthen your position**. Knowing the life stage of your specific working group and the challenges ahead will help eliminate some of the risks involved in such an ambitious undertaking.

With all of the sections moving forward, we will be openly dis-cussing how the rigor of this process applies to nonprofits in many cases. It is important to remember that this type of rigor applies to each of the four forces, just not necessarily their parent organizations. So for corporate ESG groups their maturity would be measured as the ESG subgroup of the company. And the government org involved with the coalition might just be the economic development division but not the entire local government.

Guiding Principles and First Things to Get Done

I always hate it when I read a great book that starts with fantastic ideas and potential structures but waits to give you the specifics of how to make the magic happen. I am committed to giving all of you much more than that, including this chapter. It would never be enough for me to give you a Maturity Model but never tell you how to make it work. Or discuss in general coalitions and governance but leave you wondering what next steps to take. This part of the book is meant to resolve that concern.

MATURITY MODELING

The necessary first step for each potential participant is to conduct an honest assessment of their organization's life stage using one of the established models designed to indicate nonprofit maturity.[1] The trajectory of every organization, both for- and not-for-profit, can be mapped on a maturity model. These "life stages" do not correlate to the age of the entity but to its history of growth and development.

"Organizational maturity" models describe an entity's ability to learn, adjust, adapt, and improve results. By identifying the level of organizational maturity, a board or other leadership team can address shortcomings and misalignments of resources. These insights then can be used to provide a road map for improving practices and processes, productivity, and technological efficacy. At the same time a maturity model can indicate the leadership skills necessary to take the organization to the next stage of growth impact. Advancing along the trajectory of maturity happens in stages, each advance being reliant on the establishment of sound processes in a number of areas, including finance, human resources, project management, overall organizational effectiveness, and digital maturity.

Advancing Toward Organizational Maturity

Organizational maturity models such as the example explored by Suzanne Smith[2] enable the board and leadership of any entity to plan for how and when their organization can move up to the next level of maturity. By measuring progress, your organization will have a road map that will help point your team, department, division, or entire institution to the next stage. The Lifecycle graphic offers specific definitions, actions, and outcomes that help identify where your organization currently resides on the maturity continuum in addition to laying out what reaching the next level requires.

Models such as the Lifecycle and Flywheel provide research-based guidance intended to assist organizations as they move from startup inspired by a "good idea" to organizational stability, sustainability, and real impact. There are numerous benefits to adopting such models for growth since they facilitate:

◆ Setting realistic expectations
◆ Preparing for likely challenges ahead
◆ Identifying the requisite leadership skills

Setting Realistic Expectations

Organizations motivated to make real change too often may confuse aspiration with capacity.

Taking on too much too soon without the necessary underlying resources, both human and financial, is a common recipe for burnout and failure. If your goals are not aligned with your resources, this misalignment almost certainly means no matter how great the effort, the outcomes are likely to be disappointing at best and devastating at worst.

Past experience proves that an organization is more likely to achieve its goals when it allocates resources that bring elements in line with each other. As your leadership strives to increase programs, for example, the finances necessary to support expanded efforts may lag. It's almost in the DNA of many nonprofits' organizations, for instance, to "do more with less," and while that is commendable and at times unavoidable, there comes a point at which programmatic growth unsupported by robust financial resources is simply unsustainable. Letting optimism or idealism contribute to operating on an "if we build it they will come" strategy simply doesn't work in business, government, philanthropy, and the nonprofit sectors.

The truth of this observation is most dramatically pointed out by the number of small nonprofits that annually are forced to close their doors for lack of funding. According to the National Center on Charitable Statistics, approximately 30% of nonprofits fail to exist after 10 years. Forbes reports that "over half of all nonprofits that are chartered are destined to fail or stall within a few years."[3] A recent survey conducted in 2025 by the Nonprofit Finance Fund (NFF) uncovered even more gloomy statistics.

◆ 85% of survey respondents expect service demand to increase in 2025.
◆ 36% ended 2024 with an operating deficit, the highest in 10 years of NFF's survey data.
◆ 86% said high costs due to inflation have impacted their organizations and clients.

◆ More than half of survey respondents (52%) have three months or less cash on hand, and 18% have one month or less cash on hand.

◆ 84% of respondents with government funding expect cuts to that funding.[4]

High failure rates are not limited to nonprofits, however. 2024 US Bureau of Labor Statistics reveals that **20.4%** of businesses fail in their first year, **49.4%** fail in their first five years, and **65.3%** fail in their first 10 years.[5] Honesty and transparency about the alignment of resources with goals is a first essential step in determining your organization's level of maturity, and by extension, its ability to set and execute durable strategy.

Preparing for Likely Challenges Ahead

The nature of the challenges your organization will face relates directly to its current level of maturity. For early-stage nonprofits and businesses, the initial challenge is often how to find the financial support necessary to build internal capacity and support its new work, product, or service. Later-stage organizations in government, business, philanthropy, and nonprofits may find themselves hampered by risk-aversion and complacency, continuing to operate in ways that no longer deliver maximum impact/profit or evidencing an unwillingness to pivot their operations or redesign their infrastructure as new needs emerge. Committing to impact assessment and continuous learning are ways to prevent more mature organizations from declining into irrelevance or failure. One strategy we are beginning to see is the willingness of some philanthropic efforts to "sunset" their operations. They are opting to achieve the greatest impact in a short time rather than working to preserve their programmatic funding indefinitely.

Identifying the Requisite Leadership Skills

In the corporate world we often see that the charismatic, passionate founder lacks the experience and expertise to scale the enterprise or take it public. The requisite skills for nonprofit, governmental, and philanthropic leadership also vary depending on the maturity stage and scope of the entity. By referencing what level your organization currently operates at, then looking at the challenges of next stage growth, a senior management is better able to identify the type of leadership that will be able to advance the organization. This may be the difference between the early-stage leader whose passion and idealism inspire support, and the later-stage leader whose business acumen contributes to building systems and operating a financially sound organization while maintaining a high level of passion and vision.

The maturity model framework offers an objective method for evaluating where you are and suggesting what may come next. As you consider forming or joining a collaborative effort, using this framework can suggest if you have the resources to take on the commitment a joint effort demands or if you have more capacity building and internal alignment to achieve first. There is no magic shortcut to answer these questions of capacity, but the process can be straightforward.

Engage both your leadership team and your board or advisers to individually complete an analysis of your organization using the Lifecycle chart. Once the results are in, convene a facilitated session to:

◆ build a conversation around the points of convergence and divergence, otherwise known as the "perception gap" based on our unique experiences.
◆ work to find agreement for where the organization is and where the most alignment or misalignment occurs.
◆ use the agreed-upon level as a starting place and the next level as a goal, developing either a short-term action plan or, ideally, a longer-term strategic plan to bring the organization into alignment. This will require investing in the necessary resources and a sound plan for acquiring them to propel growth to the next stage of the entity's life.

A Final Word on Maturity Models
According to Murphy & Meyers,[6] capacity building in turnaround settings depends on identifying specific weaknesses—such as decision-making, communications, or coalition strategy—and addressing them

incrementally. Maturity models are a simple tool to enable this part of organizational transformation. Maturity models depend upon agreement by the core leadership group to be guided by these objective documents in order to develop a road map for their own organization.

The model, when honestly applied, shows the current state of affairs compared to steps to be taken along the way to eventual maturity. The actual maturity models themselves, of course, can be customized for each organization as long as the output contains a specific, unique view of where individual organizations land in the model and what they need to do to improve before taking on the joint task of collaboratively building stronger communities.

COALITION BUILDING

Once the foundational work of maturity modeling is complete, it's time to build momentum through organizing. Perhaps because so much of the current public discourse describes a deeply divided society, an old adage promoting collaboration is once again being heard among emerging changemakers. "If you want to go fast, go alone. If you want to go far, go together," is a sentiment often attributed to traditional African proverbs. Contemporary research into the effectiveness of initiatives bears this out.

Hasenfeld & Garrow (2012)[7] emphasize that nonprofits advocating for rights can be more effective when allied in coalitions rather than when conducting independent, isolated campaigns.

So while coalition building is a responsibility for each Perseverance member organization, no two entities will approach this effort in identical ways. Depending on the culture, context, and constituency of each participating member, each organization will benefit from specific training conducted by folks expert in how to organize groups in the local community. Quite frequently there are community organizers already working in several of the participant groups who can serve as natural teachers for the rest of us. They may have experience doing outreach for their workplace, or perhaps as active members of other civic or social groups such as PTAs, auxiliaries, church or school groups, neighborhood associations, clubs, or sporting groups. Identifying these savvy coalition builders and tapping into their knowledge yields a terrific return.

The best part of community building training is that all the engaged individuals take home specific skills that are beneficial no matter which of the four forces you represent. Foundations, nonprofits, corporations, and governments need to have individuals skilled in building coalitions, both internally and externally. While the members of the group may change over time, what must remain constant is a group commitment to continuous coalition building. Only when each Perseverance member embraces maintaining a robust coalition of support as a core responsibility can guaranteed continual growth and effectiveness over time occur.

GOVERNANCE

You've managed to do a fine job of determining your organization's maturity level and in the process come to understand what you bring and what you lack in this coalition. After training and practice, you've begun to build awareness and support for the societal need your Perseverance group has coalesced around. The next challenge? Who's in charge?

Perseverance participants come from all four forces—government, philanthropy, corporate, and nonprofit—where, chances are, the power dynamics and decision-making processes are quite different. In addition, there are the limiting stereotypes we hold about our counterparts working in these various sectors. I don't have to spell it out. You know what I mean. But here's the hard and simple truth: for a Perseverance coalition to succeed, our biases and egos have to be parked at the door. A joint effort will only succeed when the prime directive is a commitment to outcomes, not the establishment of a ruling hierarchy.

While every one of the forces as well as each individual member bring different levels of resources to the table, the group needs to be built based upon consensus driven by the agreed-upon outcomes the group is pursuing. This requires respect, civility, and even humility. Creating a culture based on these values enables genuine collaboration. It will also protect and even encourage vibrant internal debate necessary to find the best route to impact. Governance founded on a unified motivator and grounded in the agreed-upon outcomes is most likely not only to achieve the greatest impact but also to ensure a long-lasting commitment to the Perseverance effort from all participants. Don't get me wrong, there will be irreconcilable differences from time to time, and the escalation and resolution process simply needs to be clear, rarely initiated, and agreed to before folks start devoting resources to the effort.

OUTCOME ORIENTATION

How does one arrive at the requisite specific and quantified outcome-oriented goals to be achieved by a certain date? Fortunately, there is ample advice out there. Over the course of 20 years, consultants, funders, national associations, and management support organizations have developed guidebooks and tools to help nonprofits and others develop outcome measurement systems for their organizations. In addition, there are shared standardized outcome measurement systems.[8] All too often efforts aimed at building strong communities are measured by completing certain *activities* instead of driving measurable *outcomes*. Hours spent working on a meals program, for example, do not necessarily translate into improvements in food security or health. Confusing activities as accomplishments can trap large organizations into doing a lot of actual "work" while not moving the needle. Their activities, while numerous, have not changed any underlying or systemic factors that contribute to a compromised social environment or neighborhood condition. Outcome orientation, by contrast, holds the promise that the same level of work (not the same activities) or output advances the agreed-upon outcomes of the group in measurable ways.

There are a few important dynamics to pay attention to when committing to outcome orientation:

1. *Goal Clarity*—As Wellens & Jegers (2014)[9] highlight, effective governance is significantly enhanced by goal clarity, which anchors both board oversight and staff action in shared expectations. The group must have specific and quantifiable outcomes-based goals instead of identifying the work to be done. Those goals should all be specifically time bound by realistic and agreed-upon deadlines. Milestones should be established for ensuring progress at regular intervals. These interim goals should be defined in terms of desired, quantifiable, and verifiable end-states or impacts (10% fewer food

insecure families, decrease in wealth gap of 2000 individuals, graduation rates increased by 40%).

2. *Objectives and Key Results (OKRs)*—According to Lynch-Cerullo & Cooney (2011),[10] goal-focused frameworks help organization shift from outputs (e.g., flyers printed) to outcomes (e.g., people actually served or mobilized). Tying Key Performance Indicators directly to outcome-based goals gives the group a regular and yet flexible set of tools to be able to regularly measure success. Setting regular OKRs on a quarterly basis gives your constituents guidance and updates as well as giving you flexibility to reshape them throughout the year.

3. *Outcome Accountability*—Groups hold themselves as well as each other accountable to achieving the actual outcomes, not just performing work. This avoids the continual problem of burnout when pointless activities are considered essential even though they are not moving the needle in the neighborhood. When we are held to account for actual impact or outcome, we still may feel exhaustion, but it will not be through wasted effort. With a focus on real impact, we will be better able to see what is worth our time and what is not, consequently becoming better able to see the actual impact in very real terms.

4. *Flexibility in Execution*—As Heinrich (2002)[11] explains, outcomes-based management enables public and nonprofit agencies to be more responsive and client-centered by reducing process rigidity. The teams can avoid the perpetual challenge of "doing things that way because we always do it that way." Staying very committed to the outcomes opens up a greater possibility of being completely flexible for how you achieve results. Same old, same old is not the solution. Innovation is. Changing this mindset empowers individual teams to get to their outcomes in the easiest and fastest way they can devise. Having the autonomy to design the most effective path to success is a proven way to deepen engagement and foster staff who are even more deeply wedded to the outcomes.

5. *Community Centric Thinking*—The Perseverance group's success must be characterized in terms of real, measurable,

visible, positive impact to our community, not to each of the member participants individually. The collaborators can't be interested in accomplishing goals that ONLY satisfy their internal organizational goals. Whatever outcomes we direct our efforts toward must directly benefit our community members, building strength and resilience equally.

What's the ROI of Getting Involved with this Perseverance Effort?

At the outset of any Perseverance group formation, each member will work through a maturity model for their own organization. This process enables them to see how well they are doing internally and help them understand what they have to bring to their communities' point of view. Coalition building provides a clearer idea of how the community feels and if the intended impact will have an end-state that represents a real win for them. A nonhierarchical form of governance increases the level of collaboration and commitment while adopting an outcomes-based orientation helps the community and increases clarity inside their own organizations to justify the expenditure of resources over time for real change. And the OKR structure gives everyone the ability to communicate successes regularly and clearly.

It's not surprising for skeptics to believe a Perseverance model can't be achieved in their particular region, citing historic rivalries, legendary animosities, lack of resources, intransigent leaderships, or any number of other crippling objections. I want you to take heart. What we have described here can *absolutely* be replicated everywhere.

I have done a significant amount of global work in my career, and I have found that when frameworks have principles but remain flexible in determining outcomes, these collaborative, cooperative, coalition-based efforts translate well to local communities **everywhere**. Expanding this Perseverance work internationally would take its own book to make the small adjustments across multiple regions to guarantee success. But rest assured, this work can and should be done outside of the United States.

How to Launch a Perseverance Chapter

Now that we've defined the foundational principles for Perseverance, let's explore in greater detail the specific step-by-step guidance needed to develop a Perseverance group in your neighborhood, city, state, or region.

Much of the planning needs to happen well before any such effort is announced and definitely before any meetings take place with the entire group.

STEP 1: ANCHOR

Find an organization that can act as an "anchor tenant" for the entire effort or at least is in a position to provide this organizational support through the first two years. This should be an organization that has been active in the local community for some time and is not identified as having a single or divisive point of view. They should overall be perceived as a positive or neutral force within the community. Their organizational culture should be open to and show a history of working collaboratively with other local groups, ideally among the other four forces. An ideal anchor tenant should be able to provide a comfortable, safe, and accessible place to hold meetings and donate enough money to cater meetings, etc. Access to elaborate resources is not terribly important, because over time your group may be able to rely on other members of the coalition for the additional resources.

STEP 2: TALENT

Recruit a small core of committed individuals, drawing from each of the four forces. These individuals should be in a position to represent the voice and convictions of their place of employment or engagement. A word of caution about who to approach. Typically, the person at the very top of an organization, while wielding the most power, is least able to commit time. Instead of trying to recruit the top person such as the CEO, executive director (ED) or top elected official, find their strong #2. It may be the COO or CFO, a top executive assistant, or deputy director. Identify the people who can actually get things done. Who has the ear of the top leaders? Who does the ultimate decision maker look to for advice? That's the person you want to find and get on board.

STEP 3: TARGET

Start the conversation to define the desired outcomes for the effort. Once you've hit on an area of impact, quantify it. Be as specific as possible. Don't be overly ambitious. In a program year, more than 2–3 outcomes are way too many. For a startup Perseverance group, committing to one measurable outcome is best! The Chicago Community Trust, for example, focused on the racial wealth gap over the past few years. That single focus meant that every conversation they had and every vendor they brought included an evaluation of impact on the racial wealth gap. Having a clear target gave them a deep focus their efforts had lacked before. And holding all partners accountable to their desired outcome, the impact they have generated has multiplied.

STEP 4: RESOURCES

Have that core group do an initial assessment of the local organizations that should be a part of the effort. Each leader should take care to take an initial stab at characterizing their involvement as well as what their level of commitment could be. This is first about how aligned their organization already is for this outcome. Are they already expending time, effort, and money to achieve this goal? What you're trying to determine is how much these various players have in common, how strong is their alignment, and how much they are already spending on ESG, CSR or other initiatives. Understanding their current posture helps to signify their level of alignment.

STEP 5. GAPS

Do an initial analysis of what resources will be needed to win. Characterize these resources as startup needs, ongoing operational needs, physical (office space, computers), or intellectual (software, research, marketing). Determine whether these resources should be centralized for all local Perseverance groups or need to be resourced individually. Could a big foundation, for example, offer centralized services to the grantees they support in the form of free or low-cost marketing, accounting, or other services they all need? Might it be possible to identify or create a regional hub providing sustainable services such as the shared services of a CFO?

STEP 6: DETAILS

Identify all startup resources needed and get agreement for who will provide that support. Secure your first meeting space and get all operational needs for that meeting set, including all the logistics and planning required, e.g., marketing, catering, staffing, etc.

The First Meeting and Beyond

Now that you have completed the pre-work for the group launch, it's time to execute your first group meeting. You've got a lot to cover and you're inviting busy people. Limit the time required by calling for a half-day meeting.

The first meeting might seem like an on ramp and so requiring too much focus on it could seem like overkill. Quite the opposite is true though. First impressions are vital, especially for the four forces doers and leaders you've enticed to sign on. Dedicate the time necessary to plan out the first meeting in great detail and be ready to keep it on task and on time. If you fail at this, you'll find few if any RSVPs to your follow-up meetings.

MANY KINDS OF INTRODUCTIONS

In the spirit of starting strong, devoting considerable time to introducing people and purpose effectively at this **first meeting of a community organizing coalition** sets the tone for trust, collaboration, and shared ownership. The goal is to move from *individuals and organizations* to a *collective identity*. Here's what I've found to be an effective step-by-step guide based on best practices (I'm going to use an example from my hometown):

1. Start with a brief, intentional opening that grounds the meeting in shared values and urgency.

   Example:
   "Welcome everyone. We've come together not just as individuals or leading organizations in the Milwaukee area, but as people rooted in this community. We're here to build our

communities power and to change conditions that have gone unchallenged for too long."

Amplify your opening statement with a brief story rooted in a specific local challenge that all will be familiar with. The goal here is to activate a common purpose. Begin by describing what your Perseverance group is and what it isn't. Fill in a few key points for all to understand and align to.

2. Describe the coalition's **focus**. Most importantly, stress that this is not a group working on any one specific issue, but rather an effort to make our community-building work more efficient and far more impactful. We will unite behind one particular outcome each year. It's not a group to do organized labor work or environmental sustainability. We are searching for the issue that ties us all together. It may be a racial wealth gap or even a better way to stimulate and manage volunteerism. Whatever it is, we have to agree that we'll test our ideas against what the community tells us it needs most urgently.

3. **Why now?** Be concrete about the challenges of past efforts as well as the hope and need involved with engaging now.

4. Establish our community agreements or the **rules of engagement** that the core group has already drafted in their prework. Present these as up for discussion and ratification. Once agreed upon, these become the opening declaration at the start of each subsequent meeting. Constantly reinforcing these agreements helps ensure inclusion and respect among our membership to promote the long-term sustainability of our coalition.

5. Invite everyone to make a brief **personal introduction (keep intros to 1–2 mins.)**, ideally providing participants with a framework to deepen connection. Direct each attendee to please tell the group their:

   - Name
   - Organizational affiliation
   - Why this coalition matters to you personally
   - What you hope to gain from the coalition
   - What you expect to contribute to this space

6. Use a visual or interactive tool to help members visualize the breadth and power of the group. Some examples are:
- **Common Ground Map:** draw lines between people with common causes, neighborhoods, or relationships.
- **Existing Power Model:** place organization names on the wall and link them to current or past key community issues or campaigns.

7. Governance and role expectations should be explained upfront so folks can commit early.
- Who's facilitating the coalition's work?
- Who's taking notes and keeping us on track (time)?
- How will decisions be made?

8. Preview the Road Ahead—Close the introduction section with clarity:
- What's the agenda today?
- What are the first wins or goals we're aiming for?
- How can people stay involved?

With the introduction section done, I suggest that you jump right into the work to ensure that the group stay committed to both action and efficiency when it comes to time.

GETTING DOWN TO BUSINESS

The following Big Seven agenda items are the most important things for the group to understand as they move forward together. Folks from corporate might think of this as a highly detailed SWOT analysis. The most encouraging place to begin is by identifying strengths.

1. Strengths: What resources and assets do we have as a group?
Start with where we already have pools of power in your coalition. This is a suggested framework, and you can and should make it your own. But it's good guidance and can provide some early-stage encouragement to develop a power map. Creating a **power map** with a community organizing coalition is a foundational strategic exercise that helps members visually identify who holds influence over an issue, what relationships exist, and where pressure or partnership is most needed. It turns abstract power dynamics into a practical campaign road map.

2. **Initial Goal:** What can we do in our first year?

What is the outcome, spelled out with specificity, that you would like to accomplish? What is the geographic scope of the group's first-year effort? Is one year the right time frame? This effort requires the first tough conversation because it compels everyone to prioritize issues in the relevant geography and to decide on and commit to the most important one attainable within the timeframe.

3. **Primary Decision-Maker:** Identify who outside the group holds the power to block or support your goal. This requires prioritization of all potential external decision makers. Who is the most important? Or are there multiple organizations that must buy in? If they are in government, who are they and at what level? If they are corporate leaders, who in the group has access to that powerful person? If they are in foundations, who in the group is currently funded by them or has been a grantee in the past?

4. **Map Influencers, Stakeholders, and Key Decision-Makers:** Around the central decision-makers, create a constellation of:
   • **Who directly influences them:** staff, advisers, donors, lobbyists
   • **What allies exist:** unions, faith groups, neighborhood leaders, nonprofits
   • **Are there active or passive opponents:** real estate associations, political rivals, etc.
   • **Are there "persuadables":** people or institutions who are neutral or inconsistent

Connect all of these in a hierarchical manner starting at the top with the decision makers then connecting the rest with arrows indicating different weights based on their place in the power/decision-making structure and use plus signs to indicate strength of the relationship. This will show you areas to maintain connections and areas that require an investment in relationship building or strengthening.

5. **Targets:** Plot power centers and develop prioritized targets. This is where you can visualize the combination of coalition members and outside influences in a coherent way. On a

large paper or board, use an X/Y axis to develop a clar-
ifying map:
- **X-axis:** Position on making your goal real (oppose → support)
- **Y-axis:** Level of power/influence over your goal (low → high)

Each individual or group (coalition members and exter-
nal influencers) gets plotted as a dot. This helps determine:
- Where to build pressure
- Where to deepen relationships
- Who needs to be neutralized or moved

6. **Look for Intersection:** Overlay your coalition's potential
   impact areas by mapping where your coalition has the
   following:
   - Existing relationships (regardless of power)
   - Constituency overlap (even if they are in differing forces)
   - Leverage or access

Visualizing the overlay helps allocate roles. In answering
each of these questions, be specific. Write down the names.
- Who can reach which target within the goals timeframe?
- Who can turn out for pressure actions?
- Who can flip a persuadable?

7. **Strategize:** Use the map to develop a strategy by:
   - Identifying the top five points of leverage **and when they
     should be in position**
   - Planning tactics accordingly (meetings, media, alliances)
   - Reporting out victories on a regular basis when appropriate

SOLVING THE MAIN UNKNOWN

Given all the work that has just been done by the coalition, the question remains, "Where should we focus to have the greatest impact?"
The last exercise for the day, described here in rather granular detail,
will combine all the intelligence we just gained and then leverage the
insights of the people in our local group to come up with several lists
of prioritized targets.

The group will fill out three sets of X and Y matrixes. The X-axis
will always be "Importance to the Community" and the Y-axis will be
our "Ability to Drive Impact." There will be three types of these
matrixes delivered by the end of the day.

a. First, we will develop a matrix that guides us to select three impacts to focus on for the following program year. All initiatives can be considered. But each one considered needs to be placed in the matrix by acclamation. So, the group must agree on the placement of the outcome on the matrix. The placement on the X-axis will depend on how "Important the Outcome" would be from the community's point of view. Following that placement, the group then needs to decide on the coalition's belief is on their ability to drive this particular impact. That results in the placement on the Y-axis.

b. The group then considers those items in the top right quadrant **(Deep Community Need** as well as **High Ability of the Coalition to Drive Impact)**. You should select the correct number of outcomes to focus on depending upon the capacity of your own local coalition.

c. Second, the group will decide on relationships to build in the next program year by placing identified important relationships from the earlier exercise on that same matrix. There is no limit to the number of relationships you place in the matrix, but the outcome should be similar to the outcome matrix. The group should place the relationships on the matrix and consider all of those in the top right quadrant. And then decide how many relationships they will move in the next program year from that grouping.

d. Finally, the members of the coalition will break off into subgroups based upon which of the four forces they identify with. Each of the forces will characterize the gaps they have identified for their force that are important to the community and that the coalition has the ability to drive the filling of. If each force could go through the difficult exercise of identifying their top gap to fill in the following program year, the coalition will be actively filling four gaps per year across the coalition. Done repeatedly this will create continuous improvement for the coalition targeting items most important to the community.

There are two other areas of inquiry that we should hold off on until the next meeting.

- ◆ *DUPLICATION* Are there areas or concerns receiving too much emphasis?
- ◆ *DISINVEST* Is there work that no longer needs to be done or at least can become a lower priority?

Local groups might decide to address one or both of these in the first meeting, but we generally think it will help to socialize the positive outcomes from the first meeting as a way to build momentum into these more challenging conversations in a subsequent session.

Tips for Doing the Work

Once you've got the framework, you'll need to provide some guidance for your working groups. In this last section you'll find specific suggestions to assist your group in identifying, mapping, assessing, and validating resources and needs, as well as an example of a Perseverance session.

FINDING CORPORATE ALLIES

Your group will be asking, "What companies are trying to do the right thing for our community?" There are multiple ways and places to go to find corporate allies for your coalition. Online is a highly efficient way to search for partners, but don't avoid asking for insights from your coalition partners. Community organizing often requires in-person meetings to gain the commitment of corporate leaders. Here are some suggested steps to gain corporate support for your coalition.

1. Define the type of support you seek from corporate partners.
   - Are you looking for certain corporations to provide influence over decision makers?
   - Do you need corporate financial support to back the coalition?
   - Are you seeking partners to publicly support policy outcomes for the coalition?
   - Do you need the corporate partner to engage their employees as a volunteer corps for your efforts?
2. Start your search with local business groups
   - Contact your local chambers of commerce, especially subgroups like the Hispanic Chamber or Black Chambers.

- Look into economic development organizations in local government.
- Contact industry-specific associations that may have identified policy-relevant awards or announcements that are local to the group.
3. Research CSR and ESG Reports and Disclosures
   - Search online for a company's:
   - **CSR reports**
   - ESG statements
   - Sustainability **pages on their corporate websites**
   - **CSRWeb and Just Capital websites are good places to dig deep**
     - www.sec.gov/search-filings will get you to the SEC Edgar database, which you can search for relevant search terms
4. Look through Local Corporate Philanthropy for:
   - Sponsorship of local events or nonprofits (look at flyers and websites)
   - Named donations in public spaces (libraries, schools, food banks)
   - Employer-matching programs advertised through local nonprofit newsletters

Some readily available sources include:

- ◆ Local press ("Business Journal" or Patch)
- ◆ Nonprofit annual reports or donor listings
- ◆ Local foundations that regrant corporate funds

UNCOVERING GOVERNMENTAL GAPS

As it defines its work and resources, your Perseverance group will be asking. "Which existing government programs are strong? Which are floundering?"

There are multiple ways to discover the governmental gaps in service delivery in your area. Here are a number of options. Your local coalition can decide which of these make sense to leverage for your group.

1. Hold **listening sessions** in the community you are working with. Ensure that the community's diversity is represented at the listening session to avoid false positives and negatives.

2. Perform a **Needs Assessment** among the members of the group to discover service gaps in local, county, and state government service delivery.

3. Analyze **Budget and Service** Coverage Data by reviewing:
   - City and county budgets (look at lines that continually grow or have recently been cut or outsourced)
   - Department performance reports (can be accomplished through a FOIA request)
   - Auditor reports (from local or State Auditor or Comptroller)
   - GIS service maps with gaps (e.g., health clinics, transit stops, shelter beds)
   - Audit Open Government Data Sources (Socrata or OpenGov)

4. **Interviews** with Public Sector Workers and Frontline Providers Arranging for confidential, non-threatening conversations with city employees, school social workers, and nonprofit contractors can offer critical insights into:
   - Service delivery that is so slow that it is essentially unavailable
   - Populations not served due to eligibility, capacity, or stigma
   - Geographic deserts (e.g., no public transportation to clinics)

5. Check for **Equity Disparities** by looking into:
   - Is access to services unequal?
   - Are BIPOC communities experiencing longer wait times?
   - Are disabled people unable to reach or use services?
   - Are services mostly digital with no analog (no internet) option?

6. **Common Gaps** to check for include:
   - Housing—Lack of shelters, eviction prevention, tenant legal aid
   - Mental Health—Few culturally competent, affordable therapists
   - Youth Programs—No programs in evenings, transportation issues, weekend service
   - Language Access—No interpretation or translated outreach materials

A Unique Role for Foundations

Given their resources and relative autonomy, foundations are uniquely positioned to offer support to your Perseverance group. Here are some ways in which foundations can make an appreciable difference to such collaborative efforts at bringing about significant change.

1. Convert a greater percentage of their annual grantmaking to unrestricted multiyear funding. Foundations placing time and activity restrictions on funding denies the reality that nonprofits

are better positioned to know where service dollars should go. Restricting grants to single years stops nonprofits from being able to build needed capacity and/or take on work that will take longer than one year to bear fruit.

2. Enable capacity-building grants. These grants must be designed to ensure that sustained capacity remains in place after the grant. This absolutely should include professional development and skills-based volunteering as a method to build capacity through virtual volunteering systems.

3. Support building shared infrastructure. Foundations need to enable regional shared infrastructure including real estate, computing services, marketing services, and infrastructure acquisition, promoting reduced overhead and enhanced efficiencies of scale among the nonprofits operating in the foundation's region.

4. Engage in participatory grantmaking. Move from top-down decision-making to community-led funding processes, which includes:
   • Having grantees or community members on grant review panels
   • Letting grassroots organizations co-design funding strategies
   • Using trust-based philanthropy principles

5. Eliminate unneeded funder bureaucracy by simplifying applications and reporting processes, aligning metrics with the systems grantees' use, and trusting nonprofits to define success on their terms.

Summary and What's Ahead

This chapter set out to introduce the principles and practices a change-minded group of individuals may find useful in starting a movement for positive social impact in their community. It's a lot. But it has proven to be a very, very powerful approach, helping to unite and empower disparate parties and practitioners around a shared goal.

Before going on to encourage more people to get engaged, in the next chapter I'd like to share stories of some of the courageous, innovative takers of action and makers of difference working in different geographies and on different issues today. It helps to be reminded that if you want to make the world a better place, you are not alone.

PART 3

Real-World Voices and Next Steps

CHAPTER 8

Learnings and Lessons from the Field

*"It's a failure of thought that causes everyone to suffer. . .
I presume the masses of people, regardless of income, want
an improved country and improved cities. And we have not
applied our best and brightest thought."*
**—Walter Lanier, President and CEO,
Great Lakes Urban Empowerment Solutions**

Doing research for this book provided me with the irresistible opportunity to connect with a group of superstars in the field of leadership for social impact. Some of the people I spoke with were folks I'd had the pleasure to work for and with. Others I had admired from afar. In every case, speaking with them gave me inspiration, hope, and some damn good ideas. I hope you'll have the same reaction.

These transcripts are from phone interviews conducted during the winter and spring of 2025. They have been edited for clarity and brevity.

The distinguished interviewees, appearing in alphabetical order, are:

James Doyle	Former Governor	State of Wisconsin
Ginny Finn	Chief Development Officer	Milwaukee Area Technical College Foundation
Deb Fowler	Executive Director	History UnErased
Walter Lanier	President & CEO	Great Lakes Urban Empowerment Solutions
Angelique Power	President & CEO	Skillman Foundation
Nadege Souvenir	Chief Executive Officer	San Antonio Area Foundation

"Don't Let the Government Off the Hook"
—James Doyle, Former Governor of Wisconsin

Matt:

Thanks for making some time for us today, Governor. Before we get into the power of the four forces on society, please describe your background in government.

Doyle:

After graduating from college, my wife Jessica and I spent two years in Tunisia in the Peace Corps in a small village in an oasis out in the Sahara Desert. We were really influenced by John Kennedy, who had formed the Peace Corps and said it was the greatest adventure a young American could have.

Then I went to law school, and I was pretty committed that I wanted to continue to do service-directed work. While most of my classmates at Harvard Law School went off to nice big corporate firms, I went to the Navajo Reservation and spent three years in a legal services office in Chinle, Arizona, in the middle of the Navajo Nation. When our oldest son was six months old, we realized we needed to be in a place that had services to support our new family. We came to Madison, Wisconsin, where both my wife's family and my family were.

Within about a year, I was elected district attorney of Dane County, my first political office. It was an incredible learning experience. I ran and won three two-year terms then went into private law practice for about eight years. At that point I continued to be engaged in a number of community activities and on several local boards. There's a lot of things people in private life can do to support a community.

Then I ran for and won the race for attorney general of Wisconsin, the chief law enforcement officer of the state. I was responsible for a lot of legal functions very influential in how you build a community. After that I ran for and won the race for governor and served two terms.

Since then, I've been of counsel at the Foley & Lardner, LLP. I've been on a number of corporate boards including as chairman of Fincantieri Marine, a naval shipbuilder in the northern part of Wisconsin. I'm the lead independent director of Exact Sciences, an innovative colon cancer screening company. I'm also on the board of Epic Systems, which is the biggest electronic health records system in the country.

I was on the Kaiser Family Foundation board for 10 years and served as chairman for five years. It's the leading health policy organization in the country, and Kaiser Health News is now the biggest health news bureau in the country. It's a nonprofit that pairs with for-profit news organizations because the nonprofit can do much more in-depth and long-term kind of journalism than what can be done by current journalism for-profits. They live out that really interesting mix of how a not-for-profit has worked with for-profits to dispense important information about health care to the population.

I also teach regularly. I've taught at the Kennedy School at Harvard, and I've taught at the School of Public Health at Harvard, and I teach now at the School of Public Policy at the University of Wisconsin.

Matt:

Governor, you've served in all of the four forces, so you should have some unique viewpoints for each of them. But can you talk a little bit about the good parts and the bad parts?

Doyle:

There are really good companies that do a lot of great things. There are companies that aren't so good. There are governments that are really good and effective and governments that aren't so good. There are foundations and not-for-profits that have managed to scam a lot of people, and there are foundations and not-for-profits that do wonderful work. So, like all endeavors, you're going to find good and bad. But one of the areas that I think your question leads to is about what they could do better.

Regarding how businesses and governments work together, I think that government and many people who work in government generally do not have a good understanding of what happens in the business world. And similarly, I don't think businesspeople have a very good understanding of what happens in government.

The best businesses, however, understand why the government's there and have long since learned that it's best to work along with the government and not fight it all the time. And I think the best governments realize that in the United States, the major employers are private businesses. Without a good strong economy in Wisconsin, or in the United States, you're going to have all kinds of social problems. So, the two, business and government, are very interdependent. That basic understanding is really important. Good businesses have figured it out, while others fight it all the time.

We were really at the high point a couple of years ago, where corporate America adopted ESG as a measurable investment and corporate governance. Large investors in the country were going to measure ESG just as they measure the cost of goods. Every company, when they would report out their earnings would have a section talking about what they were doing in terms of environment, sustainability, and governance. Obviously, right now, we're in an enormous fight over that. I hope we're still in that world, although the pushback from the current administration is enormous against anything like that.

Matt:

Is the technical college system a good example of this collaboration between government and business?

Doyle:

There are some aspects to our technical colleges that are somewhat unique. They have local boards and are governed in local tech systems. The local board means that local employers that need employees of a certain kind can go to their local technical college and work through what kind of training program both students and employers might need.

A really interesting company that did this kind of work is Quad Graphics, which is one of the biggest printing companies in the country. They have largely funded a Graphic Design and Printing Program at the Wisconsin Technical College. It's backed up by a lot of local property tax and state tax dollars that go to the technical college. And it's specifically designed to help a particular industry that's very important in the region. Solid collaboration between government and business.

Higher education is the area where philanthropy, state government money, and not-for-profits come together. This is where huge philanthropy dollars move the country. To watch great philanthropists come in and work with the university to do good things is a heartwarming experience. When people give hundreds of millions of dollars to universities, it sometimes raises questions such as whether the philanthropist has some say in what the program is. Sometimes the philanthropists may be going in one direction, and the university wants to go in the other direction.

There was a really good example of complicated collaboration in Madison last year when the university raised the money to help build this new football practice facility on the same block of land where the old engineering school badly needed to be replaced. For a year the government struggled to balance the need for government funding for education alongside philanthropic giving for sports and a corporate interest in engineering education. Higher education is where you see big dollars moving from philanthropy and corporations into the public sector.

We've been fortunate to have wonderful philanthropists who have worked with the university. They'll go and ask the university, what is it that you really need? This is a place where you see huge philanthropy really doing a lot of public good.

Matt:

The short-term crises that we have on a regular basis are issues such as hunger and food banks, and we've got to feed people on the streets. But there are long-term systemic changes that need to be addressed in terms of food distribution, food deserts. How should we think about balancing those things? How do we balance those with these four forces?

Doyle:

Take food, for example. I was just the co-chair of an organization trying to raise money for the River Food Pantry, which has now become the biggest food distributor. We had to raise around fourteen million dollars.

Food is a good example because people understand food and they understand hunger, and they give for that. Sometimes it's more difficult when the issue is more obscure, not quite as in-your-face as hunger or not quite as easy to get your hands around as hunger.

What you don't want to have happen is for private philanthropy to take over the government's responsibility. The government has a responsibility here, and the government can't back away and say, "Let's have private people do it." Every now and then, for example, when they talk about cutting Medicaid, you can listen to some leaders that would say, "When I was young, churches and charities took care of the people."

Well, we're living in a different world. When you have a serious illness or a chronic illness you just can't say, "I'm going over to St. James and see if somebody will raise me the money." One of the challenges, I think, is to not let the government get off the hook on what its responsibility is. And good governments and good governors should be looking at what the long-term challenges are and what the long-term strategy should be.

With regard to hunger, the real underlying issues are poverty and joblessness and education. These are the challenges that governments has to deal with. A not-for-profit can sort of lay out the economic development plan for a community, and a not-for-profit or a company could have a charter school here or there, but they can't build an education system. They can't build the health systems that can handle the huge populations of people that now come through health systems. Only governments can do that big work and that's their role.

Matt:

Let's talk a little bit about my favorite thing, which is risk-taking and experimentation. What's your take on the approach that needs to be taken to risk-taking and experimentation in the social sector? In government? In philanthropy? What's their responsibility to take additional risks?

Doyle:

I think you need a real range of not-for-profits, philanthropists and eventually government, and you need good, substantial, stable funders as well. I think there's a huge role for the risk-takers. For example, my son works for an organization called the Black Women's Wellness Foundation of Madison, and one of the things that they've been really pushing is guaranteed minimum income. Not a minimum wage, but a guaranteed income. There's a lot of data to suggest that if people aren't stressed out over just the basics, paying rent and having food, it reduces all kinds of other social costs.

There are decent, well-thought-out arguments on both sides of this. It's a good place for a philanthropist and a not-for-profit to work, to really see what the results are. As the effort grows local government could step in, say we're going to assure that everybody has a basic monthly income of a certain amount. Not that makes them rich, but they can pay for rent and pay for food. Local government has a key role here.

That kind of risk really starts as a role for philanthropy. Let's see if it works or not, get the experience so that we know what happens. It's hard for a government to do that immediately at scale. Government might pass something like this at some point if there has been data developed that it really does reduce childhood poverty, it improves education, reduces health care costs, and so on. Good risk-taking by philanthropists can be enormously helpful developing the data and the experience, then for government to come along later and fulfill its role.

Matt:

Are there any policy or regulatory changes that would improve either philanthropy or the nonprofit experience in Wisconsin or in the country?

Doyle:

In my current life, where my wife and I do donate at levels that we never dreamed we would be able to in the past, I would say the rules we operate under are favorable. 401(k) payouts, for example, are highly incentivized to make sure that those go to charitable organizations. The ability to set up a donor-advised fund is enormously helpful too. I can see both sides of this argument because, on the one hand, it's a significant loss of tax revenue to have DAFs shielded from taxes, but on the other hand, you get in return a commitment that money that I put into that fund can never go to anything other than charitable giving. I operate under a pretty good set of laws that seem to me to encourage me to do something to build strong communities. But we do need to find ways to extend that same kind of benefit to others.

Matt:

What would you say to new young leaders coming up so that they know how to drive meaningful impact in their lives, in their careers, and in their community?

Doyle:

In those early years, coming out of college, coming out of graduate school, coming out of a technical college, that's a time for you to do something impactful to your community. Nobody has to go into the Peace Corps, even though for me the Peace Corps was life changing. It set me on a course of service that I wanted to provide to the communities I cared about. I really encourage young people, don't get too hung up right away about getting the perfect job that you're going to have for the next fifty years. Go and do some things for others.

If you're working in a local mayor's office somewhere, you're probably doing some really good work for the community. And keep reminding leaders that government has an obligation in these areas.

Similarly, I applaud the companies that have social engagement efforts at their companies. One thing that I think is critical for the corporate world is to have the whole organization participate in some way or at least have the opportunity to participate. People who are working in accounting can take part in the food drive and the things that the companies do to strengthen their community, not just those working on corporate social responsibility.

I've always believed that we should have a national service requirement in the country, and for a lot of reasons. Not only do you get to provide good service, but it's a way to get to know people from other parts of the country. But at least give the population good service opportunities, which we do, like the Job Corps and Teach for America. Those kinds of opportunities are ones that I hope people really take, and governments continue to offer.

By the way, I wanted to add one thing I just wanted to focus on for a second because it's something you might want to be thinking about. The news media is really changing. Newspapers are cutting staff. Even the biggest papers—the *New York Times*, the *Washington Post*—they all had health departments, with health writers that were writing about health.

Some of them still have them, but many are just eliminated, in particular, in middle-size and smaller papers. Reporting on health just wasn't there. So, the Kaiser Family Foundation, a not-for-profit, undertook to establish a health news bureau, and they set up partnerships with major for-profit companies like the New York Times, the Washington Post, and with a lot of not-for-profits. Kaiser had long-term relationships with public radio and public TV, and they've established new bureaus, I think there are four or five in the country.

There was a lot of discussion at the Kaiser board level. "Is this what we should be doing, bailing out for-profit companies that are making this choice not to cover health like they did before?" The decision was that's part of our charter. And to the extent that those partnerships with for-profit and some not-for-profit media outlets dispense information about health systems or about health care, that's our job. The reality of the world is that this isn't getting done right now, at least not to the level it should be. And we're the ones that can go in and do it.

So, if you look at any major long-term health story that you see in the *New York Times*, the *Washington Post*, and the biggest newspapers, this all comes from the Kaiser Family Foundation. It all comes from a not-for-profit. It's an example of some public good that newspapers, in fairness to them, couldn't afford to do anymore. It's where a not-for-profit stepped in on a very large scale, a national scale, to provide a service that was no longer there in the for-profit sector.

We ended up being able to get the best reporters in the country because you'd much rather come and work for Kaiser, where you don't have to deal with deadlines. You can write things in-depth; you can really get into the studies. Plus, you have access to all the data and policy analysis that the other part of the Foundation is doing. This is an example of how the multiple forces can work together in our communities.

"Philanthropy and Foundations have Challenges but through Collaboration with Government and Corporations we can Move Forward"
—Ginny Finn, Chief Development Officer, Milwaukee Area Technical College

Matt:

Tell me a bit about your background in the philanthropic community and elsewhere.

Finn:

I'm not unusual for my generation. I sold Girl Scout cookies. I went to Catholic school and probably had to sell other stuff like at bake sales, but I didn't grow up going, ooh, I want to be a fundraiser. My original life is in the theater where I was a stage manager.

And then I married a guy with a day job, and I knew I was never going to see him if I kept being a stage manager, because he goes to the office during the day and I worked nights. So, I switched to front of house work because I still wanted to stay in the theater. That job was development or what we now call fundraising or advancement.

Eventually, I was working in the theater in San Francisco and New York City and the suburbs of New York City during the height of the AIDS epidemic. At the same time, I was volunteering because of the AIDS epidemic. That's when I decided to go to law school. So, what do you do if you were once a fundraiser, now you're a lawyer and you don't want to practice law anymore? You find a job doing planned giving. I landed at the University of Wisconsin—Milwaukee, and after that I decided to consult for nonprofit organizations.

I consulted for a little bit, not quite two years. One of my clients became my employer, a nonprofit called ABCD (After Breast Cancer Diagnosis). It allowed me to dive more deeply into the world of health care as a lay person and learn about that through the lens of the cancer world. Soon, another client became an employer, YWCA of Southeast Wisconsin. I was supposed to be the interim CEO for three months but eventually I became the actual CEO, although I negotiated a two -year contract with the board. After a new CEO was identified, I went back to consulting when several months later, another of my clients became my current employer. I now work for the MATC Foundation (Milwaukee Area Technical College).

Matt:

So given that background, you've seen it from the ground, you've seen it from the front of house, the back of house, you've seen it from the development side, and you've seen it from the executive side. Describe the current state of philanthropy as you see it. Philanthropy, not just nonprofits.

Finn:

The state of philanthropy, the state of doing things for the benefit of someone else, is as imperfect as it's always been, except that I think we have this odd paradox going on. We are both more honest and more dishonest about that disarray than in the past. I think part of the issue is an age old problem. You can't fix a problem if you don't agree on what the problem is.

It's really interesting that a country so embraces capitalism and says the consumer is king, yet when it comes to things that are funded philanthropically or through government grants I think the failure to listen to the people who are experiencing what it is you're trying to fix is a big historical failure. And I'm hopeful that at least in some sectors that is changing a bit. I really think a kaleidoscope of perspectives is actually necessary to solve complex problems.

At least the people with money and power to some extent are actually listening to some of the people who are actually mired in the problem through Trust Based Philanthropy.

Matt:

How have you seen the nature of philanthropy change over the arc of your career?

Finn:

A lot of things have changed.

People knocking on their neighbor's doors asking for money for the Easter Seals is not new. I've been around long enough that everything old is new again. I do think there are a couple of things that are dramatically affecting philanthropy that are recent. During President Trump's first administration in 2016, he changed the tax code. There was a dramatic dip in philanthropic donations due to the increase in the permissible standard deduction that corresponded with a decrease in the number of households making charitable contributions especially in that small to mid-range. That dip occurred before COVID showed up.

That dip to me sends a message to people who are promoting investment and donations to their organizations. If you spent all your time saying people should donate because they get a tax deduction, then you have given up the opportunity to really talk about why your work is important. Certainly, tax structures matter, especially with large and complex donations. But if that is the primary motivator, then you're not doing a good job, fundraisers, in getting the message out of why the work is important. When you write a check because you get a tax deduction, I'm not talking to you about the power of education or the importance of whatever the issue is.

Another change, which has only accelerated in the last eight years or so, is the concentration of wealth. This has real consequences for philanthropy. The axiom has always been that 20% of the people give you 80% of the money, but it is so concentrated now that you can go to a seminar and they'll tell you to stop paying attention to people who can't give you more than $10,000. They'll say this depending on what your mission is, the size of your organization, etcetera, but that's absolutely mind boggling to me. Because the reality is it's not just about the size of a check, it's about making sure you're educating the community writ large about the importance of your issue.

Another thing, which is not new, but has grown, is a function of wealth accumulation in donor-advised funds. On one hand, I think there's a real philanthropic benefit to donor-advised funds, especially for those who are in a position to make planned gifts. They can provide money philanthropically at a time where it works for their tax structure and their estate planning and the other things that matter to their life. That's all good. But the idea that the money can sit there and not have to do good, but the donors already enjoyed the benefit of the tax benefit, that's a broken social contract. Where's the public benefit in that? Part of the tax structure that should be looked at is a way that encourages donors to continue to use that tool but encourages spending those funds in a timely manner so that people are fed and educated.

Matt:

Talk to me about some of the systemic challenges as well as positive trends in philanthropy.

Finn:

You know, in a for -profit business, if money is tight, if revenue is down, the last thing you do is tie the hands of the sales department. Yet too often foundations are so under-resourced, it's a wonder they are making progress, even incremental progress, in terms of both the tools that are available, the staffing that's available, and the training that's available for ongoing professional development.

I'm pretty darn lucky. I work with amazing people, both volunteers and my paid colleagues, but it's clear that for some of the folks that we admire the resource allocation to the development function is quite different. I understand it's always a "push me, pull you" dynamic with the development department. Whatever services are being delivered are not perceived as a service. Part of that is, I believe, the fault of Charity Navigator and the Better Business Bureau. They created the narrative 20 years ago that administrative overhead was a problem. And I'm sorry, if you can't pay your electric bills, if you don't have appropriate computer equipment, if you can't actually give even basic health insurance to your employees, then yeah, forget it. And what's interesting to me is they created this myth, and now they've all issued a joint white paper which basically says administrative overhead IS necessary, and a random percentage isn't going to tell you whether or not the mission's being effectuated. But of course, it hasn't gotten the same traction. So, there are logical, programmatic, mission -related reasons to have high administrative costs. And I have never seen consistent messaging from the for -profit sector about what's an appropriate distribution of their administrative costs in order to get their work done.

Especially given the current climate we're living in, the concept of trust-based philanthropy is making some real progress. This doesn't mean there is no accountability in the sector. But it does mean that a funder who isn't a mental health expert is not going to tell a funded organization that is a mental health provider how to do their work. They're going to ask, "What is the right way to provide funding?" It means there is created an actual sense of partnership so that if things don't go according to plan, you're willing to talk about it.

That's really what trust-based philanthropy is. I think that historically funders were looking for that new, innovative solution that the community has. But funders wanted to have proven results because they don't want to risk their money. And that's the challenge and opportunity.

Funders also want copious reports that aren't really serving any purpose other than data collection. All of a sudden, the funded charity is turning into the funder's research office and not being compensated for that. If you have some trust as a funder, you can actually figure out how to benefit the larger cause if you stop micromanaging and mandating those kind of things.

Matt:

There are well-meaning philanthropists who want to spend their time unilaterally on solving the big problem and don't want to worry about the daily challenges on the street. Then there are nonprofits on the front lines trying to make sure that people don't starve every day. Multiple parts of this society need to work together instead of against each other. What are your thoughts about that?

Finn:

Mostly what I see is all the really complex social issues are tied into economic mobility. Because the reality is, with at least baseline economic mobility, we can make choices. And we can't choose how to be environmentally conscious if we don't know how to feed ourselves. We can't learn about our world that is changing very quickly unless we have some fundamental education, those kinds of things. I can give you an example of how things don't yet work perfectly together but are moving in the right direction at my current job.

Metropolitan Milwaukee has really horrible economic statistics for a large portion of our population. We have one of the most extraordinary technical and community college systems in the nation. We have a workforce gap. We've got employers that are just desperate for workers. We have plenty of potential workers, both un—and underemployed, and young. And in our community, we're looking at a retirement cliff in every industry, from office workers to factory workers. A lot of these industries are changing so quickly, you cannot go from high school and just get a job anymore. Not one that's going to be family supporting. What the college does and the MATC Foundation therefore supports, is a solution to that problem. In particular, community college is still not accessible for the vast majority of those who are un—and underemployed. The absence of financial support for them to go to school is a problem. We've seen this happening nationwide.

The reality is if you want people to graduate with an education that prepares them to go to work on day one you have to financially support them as generously as possible. You do not give them $500 when their semester tuition is $3,000. You give them the entire tuition. You make sure they have money for their books or their supplies. At MATC we're starting to have that conversation because we had a donor who very generously focused the money that way, provided a two-for-one challenge, and then said, "I want this to go to work right away." So every time we raised $500,000, we got a million. They didn't wait for the match to be fully done. The results have overwhelmed the donor family. They're just so pleased.

The other thing goes back to the tax code. This isn't just about the 501(c)(3) tax code. Any financial support you give to a student that isn't a direct academic expense for tuition, books, whatever, the rest of any financial support is considered taxable income. Room and board students get when they go to a residential college; that's not an academic expense. If you're already living paycheck to paycheck, if a grant doesn't support transportation, or supplement food, you're going to still work and go to school part-time. You can't go full-time because you need to put food on your own table. In most community colleges in this country, the students are adults [who are] probably responsible for putting food on the table in your family. So Government has an integrated role to play.

Matt:

Organizations that are effective generally know their role. Government must know its role and also understand how they work with others.

Finn:

The Wisconsin state legislature and the governor, obviously controlled by two different parties, recently did get their role and that was wonderful. We happen to be in a state that has a huge problem with getting access to a dentist. This dentist shortage is in our central cities and in every rural area in the state.

It's not because there are not enough people interested in being dental assistants or dental hygienists. It's that no college in the system, no technical college in the system had the physical capacity to have more students. We have waiting lists. The state legislature and the governor signed legislation right away, a special allocation for the sole purpose of having interested campuses use the money to build out more physical capacity for dental assistant and dental hygienist training. There was a private match enabled by us and the dental industry was interested in contributing to the cause.

Before the legislation ink was even dry, we were already in negotiations with two foundations of the two biggest dental businesses in the state. They decided the need was so great for them as a business, as well as recognizing that these foundation folks are people who live in our community, who work there, and who want good things for their community. They didn't limit the funding to just one school. They provided funds to be used in every campus that was taking the legislature up on this allocation. This is an example of something that worked really well.

Matt:

This is a powerful example of a state that is arguably purple being able to come together on a question that impacted all of the state's citizens. The only way the need could be addressed was with a combination of public funding, of private funding and corporate matches.

Finn:

And there's the private individual. Primarily individual funding has come in because you can create all this, but if people can't afford to enroll, what difference does it make?

"When Foundations Understand Nonprofits and Governments Partner with us, the Community gets Stronger"

—Deb Fowler, Executive Director,

History UnErased

Matt:

We're going to start with some basic background. Describe your background in philanthropy and nonprofits, including what led up to your current role and what your current role is.

Fowler:

I was launched into the education space in 1988, when I was dishonorably discharged from the United States Army. I was a Korean linguist and had orders to report to the DMZ with a top-secret security clearance. Well, let's just say it was an ugly experience. But there's never an ill wind that doesn't blow some good. So, I ended up teaching in South Korea for several years and discovered that I loved teaching.

Subsequently, I taught for more than a decade, working with new immigrant and refugee populations of students. I produced a couple of documentary films while in the classroom to highlight students and families who have been ignored, marginalized, or excluded from the public education sphere.

This experience, over the course of several years, led me to co-found History UnErased, an education nonprofit whose mission is to put LGBTQ history in its rightful place in the classroom. By "the classroom," we mean mainstream US history, civics, and social studies. We aim to bring a more inclusive, accurate reflection of the story of America to all students.

We were officially founded in 2015 by me and a former colleague, Miriam Morgenstern. To date, we have partnered with around 3,000 schools in eighteen states that are now teaching our curriculum in their mainstream courses, from K-12 schools. We've partnered with the New York City Department of Education, and our work there is funded through the New York City Council. We've been working there for the past seven years, with an ongoing grant cycle.

But we've just recently instituted our single teacher license, which I'm sure we will touch on later. There are way too many egregious bills circulating in state legislatures, restricting what can be taught in our K-12 classrooms. Our single teacher license puts the power in teachers' hands. Since we instituted that, our curriculum is now being taught in states such as Texas, Florida, Tennessee, Utah, Missouri, South Dakota, Arizona, Alabama, and New Mexico.

So, it is working around the hurdles. Previously, when we would partner with K-12 schools, the prospecting process was a glacial pace of years. We just needed another avenue to move our mission forward.

Matt:

No single organization or sector can make progress in the United States; we need to work collaboratively. Your organization is a great example where you have worked directly with local units of government. But talk to me about how local government units got involved. What can local units of government do to engage with organizations like yours across the country?

Fowler:

I love that question. As History UnErased is a 501(c)(3) education nonprofit, it's a delicate relationship sometimes with local governments or state governments. But one avenue that is really helpful and impactful is for local governments to reach out to philanthropic opportunities within those communities to help support, not 100%, but to help support in a 50/50 partnership model, bringing us into that particular school community.

The investment by local government is a nominal amount. Frankly, it's not much; schools could have a bake sale and raise that amount of money. But having everybody on board is crucial. So local government entities can take on a leadership role, and that's very powerful because they're elected officials.

Matt:

It's very interesting that you've opened up a single-user license for individual teachers. Can you describe what that looks like? So that teachers who read the book know what they can do?

Fowler:

Teachers are seeking out additional resources, primary source-based resources, from trusted entities. The single teacher license is honoring that. It is honoring those teachers who are taking a risk, but it's a risk that is worth taking. And that's what we hear over and over again. I do want to circle back to one thing which is super important with a single teacher license. And that is that the training and the support is key. The way that we're offering that to single teacher license holders is office hours every week and monthly programming. We stay tethered to those teachers who are teaching the curriculum, no matter what the structure is or how we got there.

Matt:

Public policy folks need to get educated about what they can do to create the community that we want moving forward. I know everyone needs to be careful about advocacy and walking that fine line, but what public policy changes would benefit your efforts?

Fowler:

So many. I'll start by saying that educational policy efforts need to include educators in the policy writing process. So often, most of the time, educators are left out of the system of policy writing. It is hugely important to bring those experts into the fold to create policy that would help History UnErased. And this is part of what we're doing—we're not an advocacy organization, but a portion of what we're doing is to petition state boards of education to restore history, civics, and social studies as a critical core discipline. We're going to start pushing now to have it tested as a matriculation requirement for graduation, and that it is LGBTQ inclusive. It may seem like a pipe dream right now, but we are going to get through this together with policy makers at all levels.

Matt:

There are corporations out there that care about what we're talking about. Can you talk about any experience you have in partnering with corporations to get some of this work done?

Fowler:

We have a wonderful partnership with New England Bio Labs, and the way that partnership happened is we provided a lunch and learn session. They loved it, they learned a great deal, and the way that we operate our corporate brown bag is a history mystery challenge. It's fun, it's interactive, it's multimedia, it's engaging. Everybody walks away having fun and learning a lot of really exciting history that they've been deprived of, and they're shocked that they hadn't learned about it.

That eventually led us into receiving some corporate sponsorship, including funding from one arm of our sponsors that fund our intro videos to some of our case studies and units. New England Bio Labs employees provide the narration for these videos, so they are contributing their literal voice to some of the content. That content is out there reaching millions of students across the country. That's been really exciting.

Matt:

Amazing. I'm assuming that you've got some relationship with some foundations that are supporting you or some other organizations that are supporting you. Can you describe that and how that relationship could work better for your organization?

Fowler:

We have some funders, but not enough, and we have been struggling to find more. We're a bootstrap nonprofit, scratching and clawing. It's tough to sell the long game of our mission and our work. People like the flashy, shiny object, and it's hard to get an audience with the right funders who are going to see that we have a great opportunity. There was an opportunity that was advertised somewhat recently.

The Melinda Gates Foundation was putting out this big amplification of the fact that they had funding for small nonprofits. Now, these "small nonprofits" had to have had annual revenues of a million to 3 million for the past four years. Now, our 990 is right around $800,000. We get a lot of work done with very little money, and I found that amplification to be offensive because I know other tiny nonprofits that are doing great work and having a tremendous influence on our communities, operating underneath that million-dollar mark. That's so frustrating.

Matt:

About 30% of the nonprofits in the country are operating on less than $200,000 of annual revenue and still having an incredible impact. Imagine what could happen if we had funding that actually addressed them.

Fowler:

Absolutely. From the start, our annual operating budget has totaled $3.4 million. That is to be able to staff this organization the way it needs to be and deserves to be, for us to have regional offices so that we can be responsive in real-time. It's not fluffy; that is bare bones right now. And this is important to note: there is an unfortunate expectation in our society that educators and artists work for free. It's horrifying.

So, even today, there is the assumption that people who are affiliated with this organization are volunteers. No, everybody is an educator, and everybody is paid. They are not paid enough, but well enough that it's commensurate with what they would be making if they were in the classroom or another office.

Matt:

We are very much trying to lift up the ethic that nonprofits should not be simply getting the scraps at the table and should not have a scarcity mindset. The idea is that nonprofits operate, in many ways, the same as corporations, but the goals they have are so much more important than simple profit. I don't have a problem with profit, but I do have a problem with the best of the best going to one group and whatever is left over going to these organizations that are literally fighting hunger, homelessness, and inclusion throughout the country. I'm very glad to lift up organizations like yours that believe we should get paid for what we do and get paid the right way.

When it comes to individual donors, are you seeing a difference in the way that donors are approaching you right now? Are you seeing fewer donors? Are they giving less? Are they giving more? What does it look like from a donor landscape?

Fowler:

It seems there is a paralysis right now.

From my vantage point, on what we're seeing unfold, it seems people have paused to see how things are going to shake out within these first 100 days of the new administration as far as where dollars need to be spent in order to put out fires. I think sadly, there's going to be an expectation to put out fires as opposed to looking at long-term strategic efforts.

Matt:

So, how do we balance? How do we fight that fight on a balanced basis? We do need to feed people who are starving right now, but we need to solve the problems of food deserts and poverty. How do we do that balance from your perspective?

Fowler:

Education is key. The process of K-12 education exists so that people can recognize when appropriating funds to put out these fires is happening at the same time that we need to invest in the long term to know what we can be avoiding. But I think we're all struggling with how to answer the question.

Matt:

One of the things that seems to make a difference is organizations understanding risk-taking and experimentation to drive programs forward. How do you view risk-taking and experimentation, especially now?

Fowler:

I would say it's time for people to put the stake in the ground and be abundantly clear about what we all stand for and demonstrate that we are willing to take risks to be successful. Yes. I think it's vitally important.

Matt:

Talk to me a little bit about how your group engages the communities that you serve in the decision-making process say, specifically with the LGBTQ+ community?

Fowler:

We take advantage of any and all opportunities to engage the community, whether it is a virtual opportunity or an on-site opportunity. We have contributed to conversations in many different spheres. The partnerships that we've developed with different colleges of education and institutions have been gateways to reach more community members.

And whether that's parents, caregivers, families, young people, or corporate entities, it's all over the map and important. Because what we're talking about is new information for absolutely everyone. And everyone, History UnErased and the community, walks away feeling. . . maybe enlightened is too strong a word, but inspired, I should say.

Matt:

If you had a magic wand, what would you like to see? Philanthropy, foundations, corporations, governments working together? How? How should that ecosystem evolve in order to be more responsive and more effective?

Fowler:

What I have experienced and witnessed is not unique. I've talked about this with other founders and Executive Directors. There seems to be a treasure chest of opportunities with potential donors, foundations, and funders. And there are a few people who have the key to facilitate introductions. There is roadblock after roadblock for smaller nonprofits such as History UnErased to connect with funders that we know will be excited to learn about the mission. It just seems like there certainly have to be guardrails, but it just seems to be a barricade that's unfriendly.

Matt:

What advice would you give to a new soldier who finds herself placed in the middle of this chaos? Especially, what advice do you have for new leaders looking to drive meaningful impact like you've been able to do?

Fowler:

To trust your instincts, to trust yourself. There's so much misinformation and attempts to cloud perceptions. Patience, persistence, perseverance, trust your intuition, trust yourself, and work hard. Don't be afraid to work hard; it's good for the soul.

Matt:

This has been a great conversation, but what have we missed?

Fowler:

For nonprofits concerned about foundation leaders, my humble opinion is to speak with them.

For foundations, they need to trust the people they are investing in. These hurdles of reports are important, yes, but don't mire small nonprofits in reporting when they should be out in the field doing the actual work of what the foundations are actually funding.

There's a lot of data that can be gleaned from small samplings. Foundations don't need to ask small nonprofits to do this weird, extensive calculus.

Matt:

I would be extremely happy to get organizations to understand that there are people on the ground who know what they're doing, and they're the ones who can make the operational decisions, and they will spend the money wisely. Let's have unrestricted funds go to them.

Fowler:

Well, Matt, thank you and I appreciate your vision and intention for writing this book. Right on, right there with you. Soldier on.

"The Lack of Coordination among the Four Forces must end and Philanthropy needs to be in Direct Touch with Who is Being Served"
—Walter Lanier, President and CEO, Great Lakes
Urban Empowerment Solutions

Matt:

In general, describe your background and what led you to your current roles in Philanthropy.

Lanier:

Long story short, Walter Lanier, lawyer, private practice for a decade and some change. Went into education for 13 years at MATC, local community college. Around the same time I went into MATC, I became a pastor of a church. I'm in my 14th year pastoring the Progressive Baptist Church of Milwaukee. And I've spent my entire professional career striving to make a difference and have impact in community, primarily Milwaukee, but with some interest in the Great Lakes region, because I was born in Buffalo, New York, and lived in Detroit, Michigan.

All of that Rust Belt challenge, the industrialized cities, high segregation, high racism, etcetera, that's been the story of my life. I am always striving to make a change, and that's what brings me to where I am today. I lead an organization called GLUE, Great Lakes Urban Empowerment Center, that strives to bring together thought leaders in that region to make a difference and have impact in our communities.

Matt:

From a public policy perspective, what kinds of changes in public policy could help your organization drive the impact you're trying to accomplish?

Lanier:

Part of what I want to accomplish is to move public policy. In Milwaukee, which is what I know best, we do not have a strong public policy framework that is attentive to community with regard to the impact that public policy is supposed to have.

There needs to be a better public policy framework that is responsive to community, that is responsive to citizens. There's a significant disconnect. I just don't think we have a strong community-focused public policy mechanism here in Milwaukee and Wisconsin. It's improving though. I think that our current County Executive, David Crawley, is a pretty good policy guy. At the state level, it's obviously very partisan, so there's not great policy coming out of there. The city is sluggish as it pertains to policy, so I wouldn't lift any particular initiative, except for the shared revenue initiative in Milwaukee. But overall, we don't have a strong public policy framework in Wisconsin. It is not very citizen informed.

Matt:

Any thoughts on how these four forces, foundations, nonprofit organizations, government, and corporates can better work together to support communities in need of strength?

Lanier:

I do a lot of nonprofit, philanthropic, or community serving stuff through my church. And it has surprised me, shocked me, disappointed me that there is not further coordination among these forces because, from my lens, it's the obvious thing to do. You know, my undergraduate degree is in finance. And when you think about how financiers come in and fund things, there's different types of financing for different functions in an entity. Each one of these four forces, the corporate, the foundations, the nonprofit, the government has a piece of a puzzle to play to solve social ills and their support and money should come in differently.

What is government money best to use for? What about foundation money? Nonprofits really don't have any money, you know, depending on what nonprofit it is. And then how does the corporate funding and support come in? When we look at a city like Milwaukee, where the social ills and challenges have an impact on every sector and everybody wants them to be better, it befuddles me that we have not figured out how to work together effectively with their resources for a whole bunch of reasons.

Matt:

MATC is just one example of technical colleges everywhere in the state of Wisconsin. Is that a functional model that we can now take from education and place it on top of things like social justice to figure out if there's a role for the four forces to play, to solve some of our biggest problems?

Lanier:

Short answer is absolutely yes. It's a preexisting model. It has all of the elements. The interests are aligned. The stakeholders need to strive toward a high degree of excellence in the model. And that's a missing piece of the puzzle.

As part of the money culture of this city and region, not understanding that you have to spend money to make it is a shortcoming. Too often things are done on the cheap and you just wouldn't do it that way if you were doing it like a business and trying to maximize the moving of metrics.

The corporate sector, who needs consumers and employees, invests much more in that ecosystem because out of that ecosystem comes both consumers and employees, but this seems to happen in a reactionary way in philanthropy.

We need to know what it means to build a system to get the outputs that you want. I think that's one of the challenges in philanthropy that there are an insufficient number of systemic thinkers at the leadership tables that understand the totality of the ecosystem. Things come in a not well-coordinated way, and therefore they do not yield the outputs that they could. But going to your first question, it's absolutely true that MATC, and the technical college system, has great potential in the place that it sits because it is an intersection of all of those component parts, the four forces.

It's important that funders have a connection to the ground and has been well informed by the people it serves. But there's a top-down design that takes place in the nonprofit ecosystem without the input of those who are served. And, by definition, you now have a flawed design.

Matt:

I'm a large advocate for a trust-based orientation. Talk to me a little bit about the history of that. How has philanthropy done a top-down approach, of hopefully years gone by, sort of dictating to a community what that framework would be? And then talk to me about more of a trust-based relationship between the community being served and the funders working with that community. How should that work? How should that be structured?

Lanier:

I want to stay focused on calling it a design thing. I'm thinking about Steve Jobs and you see periodic random quotes from him. One of the ones that sticks out to me is, designing with the customer or the end user in mind. Everything is about serving that customer. That's business wisdom. And he executed that relationship with the customer well.

On the other hand, I've been in nonprofits and served on boards in finance, education, public health, mental health, social justice. In every one of those sectors, communication with the end user happened at the end of a process. I've been on boards where we had a discussion about how to design a solution, the problem they're trying to fix. And usually as an add-on at the end, if at all, there's a comment like "we need to talk to the student" or "let's talk to the client" or "let's talk to the customer" or "let's talk to the patient" as kind of an appendage to a process that's already taken place. And that is a flawed design.

It's not only that it is a good thing to do or moral thing to do; it is the correct business practice. It's a correct design function. It's illogical to think that you're going to solve for somebody but you've not heard from them. It's very paternalistic or maternalistic. But moreover, you wouldn't do that in a business, you wouldn't be effective in a business environment. You wouldn't have a competitive advantage if you were not continuously hearing from the market that you serve.

And so, it **is** trust-based. That is a way to frame it. That's important. That's understood in the community. And I just want to layer on top of that. It's good business.

When we bring a "business" approach to the philanthropic sector, wouldn't this be one of the first great things to ask? What does the customer say? What does the consumer say? What does the student say? There's a 10-year project, "M-cubed," going on right now in education. And I've been beating them on the head to make part of their project, listening to what the students say. There's no student voice. And the outcome they want is improving outcomes for students. And they have nothing in this plan a decade later. The project is a combination of UWM, MPS and MATC. And the second challenge is, how about some equity goals? Any equity goal, just one. Can we identify one? And they haven't done it.

Whoever gets their mind around the trust-based, "hearing from the market and the consumer or the student" will have a significant competitive advantage. Whoever moves in that direction, especially in these Rust Belt cities where you have high degrees of segregation, will have a significant competitive advantage.

Matt:

All right, let's move in a different direction. What's going on with donors? When you talk to donors in your role as the head of a big nonprofit or at MATC or at GLUE, what's the conversation that's happening out there? What are their concerns? What are the things we have to pay attention to?

Lanier:

There are both good and challenging things with donors. There seems to be a desire for increased accountability from them. They want to be more accountable as donors, and they are looking more at impact. They need to look inward first.

Funders are asking, what is our impact? They think they need to do a better job of tracking actual impact. And there's an impulse to go to those who are being funded and drive that accountability down and say, you got to increase **your** accountability because now **we** are being more accountable. So, we're going to impose more paperwork on you. Rather than saying, okay, let us evaluate ourselves.

How did foundations get to this place where we were not actually being impactful and then not overreact and turn our ineffectiveness and now impose constraints on those we're funding. How did we miss this? What does this say about us? What culture shift do we need to make in our foundation rather than a process shift forced on our grantees? We've got to impose more accountability, but it's got to serve an end. And if the culture is not right, then the additional processes would just be more constraining.

I saw funders start some of that shift. We created an organization called the Milwaukee Black Grassroots Health Equity Network about six months into the pandemic. We went to a large Milwaukee based foundation for some funding and we were going back and forth. But then they were kind of engaged in pushing down accountability. They were imposing some stuff that was nonsensical given what was happening in the moment, which was the pandemic. And so we pushed back on them pretty hard.

And after the pushback, Zilber was responsive, and they pivoted, and they shifted how they worked with us in that moment and then funded the effort. I then said to our team, revisit what happened with Zilber and talk about the process from their side. What did **they** hear? What caused **them** to transition and work with us in a way that understood both what the impact they were striving to get and the current reality of the community given the pandemic. This anecdotal moment of them being deeply responsive to the community voice and having some trust helped both of us drive impact.

Matt:

The bottom-line question is, do you think philanthropy with its $1.8 trillion of endowments is spending enough of their money on solving the problem?

Lanier:

No, I don't. Philanthropy has to do some risk-taking as well. An excellent CEO in the for-profit corporate sector understands risk, understands decision-making, understands the dispatching of capital for different reasons, how to quantify for risk, how to reserve for risk. Foundations have to be more risk-averse, but must not operate without risk, because if we do that, it'll be centuries before we see impact. That's where the coordination would make a difference. When people say to nonprofits that they need to operate like a business, it's a very simplistic statement. I think if foundations could underwrite a sliver of risk, to allow nonprofit CEOs to be a bit more risk-takers and to fund them to connect more with the communities they serve, then the system would be better. Foundations may need to tap deeper into that $1.8 trillion to accomplish this.

Matt:

The 5%, "limit" that endowments believe they are under with regard to spending their endowments is in actuality not a limit, it is a floor. Any thoughts about the 5% rule and whether that could be augmented a bit?

Lanier:

With regard to the 5% rule, when you said it was people treating it as a ceiling rather than a floor that tells you everything you need to know, know—it's not functioning the way it was designed and therefore a whole wave of capital that could be dispatched is not dispatched. If you're looking from a business model perspective, you would point to that and say, "here's a problem." This whole layer of the system is undercapitalized and you have to wonder, why?

Is there somebody overcapitalized? This structure results in foundations sitting on all this capital. I remember well from my education; you can actually have too much capital. And when you do, it's going to waste. You might as well dig a hole in your backyard and toss it in there. Dispatch that capital so it can produce some outcomes.

Matt:

When I discovered that there was $1.7 trillion sitting in endowments, I wondered, if you're not going to let us spend it more than 5% per year, let us lever it. Let us borrow against it. Guess what? In most of the states, that's not legal. Large nonprofits and foundations aren't allowed to borrow against their endowments in many states. Please don't hurt poor people because we can't lever those assets. Those financial tools like leverage that wealthy families use need to be available to all of us.

Lanier:

A lot of the stuff I look at through this lens of lawyer plus finance plus pastor. It's a nice mix because there's a better way to do this. And there's a discipline around it. And there's a history of doing it successfully, just saying the same thing you're saying.

And then we know as lawyers, at least as private sector lawyers, you don't tell people what they can't do. You try to figure out how can we counsel them to do what they want to do. That's a different frame of mind. And that's what we should be doing.

Matt:

Walter, is there anything else you want to add?

Lanier:

It's a failure of thoughtful engagement that causes everyone to suffer unnecessarily. I presume the masses of people, regardless of income, want an improved country and improved cities. And we have not applied our best and brightest thoughts to this part of the world.

"Listen to your Community and Empower the Youth to Lead"

—Angelique Power, President and CEO, Skillman Foundation

Matt:

How are things going with Skillman in Detroit?

Power:

Things are going well, I mean, everything requires that we view our work through our values now more than ever. So, we are in a really good place with this strategy that had been co-created with so many. I was saying to my staff and to the board, if we had not had a strategy that was focused on being very community-rooted and working on policy and systems change, given everything that is happening, we would have to figure out that strategy now.

We actually have a head start on having built trust. I recently left a monthly gathering of community members that we host in our hub called Common Grounds—this one was on immigration.

We just open the floor and open the doors and listen. And folks come from all over. I feel like we are in alignment with what our purpose is right now, and we're kind of trained up to respond in this moment, not from a place of hubris and not from a place of being frozen with fear, which I'm sensing from a lot of folks.

But to just keep moving in alignment with what we know we're meant to do and to try to be open to this moment. There are possibilities and it's hard to see that when the change happening right now is just so aggressive and beyond our control. And it's often mean-spirited, and it feels like angry policy. But, you know, we needed a disruption, and this is definitely a disruption. There have been these plans for new policy changes that have been in the works for a really long time across a range of constituents. And we're just kind of getting focused on what we do now in this disruption and what we know and then remaining open to what possibilities this changing world might offer.

Matt:

Yeah. I see the community sort of getting back to some of its core principles. We had gotten away from community organizing for a while, and this may be forcing us to do it. I want to give you this platform to be able to tell the world what Skillman is doing, what Detroit is doing, what Michigan is doing, and what Angelique is doing to make that all happen.

Let's start with just general background. Tell me about how you got to Skillman and your background before Skillman.

Power:

Well, I never grew up hearing the word "philanthropy" as an institutional sector that moves capital in a certain way. But I certainly grew up understanding mutual aid and what philanthropic communities look like and what it feels like to be a part of them. I think that my first interaction with philanthropy was growing up on the South Side of Chicago, growing up in a family that is Black and Jewish, and being the daughter of a public-school teacher and a Chicago police officer.

Without even knowing it before I stumbled into this profession, which I certainly stumbled into, I was grounded in community and especially having a public school teacher and a police officer as parents being aware of these professions that are often dealing with the symptoms of very broken systems. This led to great and important dinner table conversations about a lot of that. I formally entered the philanthropic sector when I was in graduate school, getting an MFA at the School of the Art Institute of Chicago (SAIC), and I was working to put myself through grad school. I took a job as a part-time assistant in the public affairs department of Marshall Field's, which was right down the street from SAIC. I would run between classes, and that was actually the first time I learned about corporate philanthropy, as this was part of the work of the public affairs department at Field's.

My first lesson came when I was making xerox copies of things and reading grant proposals while the machine ran. I had decided to, in the process of making all of these copies of grant proposals, to put my own recommendation on the proposals. I would write on a post it "Yes, it should be funded" or "No." And I brought it to my boss, who humored me and basically challenged my idea, asking me about financials and the last grant and all of that. It's funny because she just published her first book, and she was on the Today Show yesterday, and I was watching her. Her book is about leadership. She has a chapter in her book about our relationship from her perspective. She truly became my first mentor, and like all great mentor relationships it really changed both of us. But all of that is my very early experience in philanthropy, specifically corporate philanthropy.

I was at Target Corporation for, I think, in total seven or eight years, learning corporate philanthropy on a massive scale. I've always been a writer and have that art school kid in me, so I never really felt like a company was where I belonged, but I got a huge kick out of it.

I left there and worked for an art nonprofit, and then I went back to philanthropy. But in the foundation space, first at the Joyce Foundation where I got my sea legs in policy and the private foundation space, then later running the inimitable Field Foundation in Chicago where we implemented a racial equity focused strategy and really began doing such innovative funding, and then in 2021 Skillman really captivated me and brought me into my current chapter. Skillman approached me in the middle of COVID, and I loved my work at Field Foundation and truly had never seriously considered leaving Chicago. But there was so much calling me to come. First of all, I love Detroit. I love that it is this city of possibilities, that it is a majority Black and Brown city, and that it feels like a place where things can get done.

I like that it's in Michigan. Michigan's a purple state. That means you have to actually work across sectors and across ideologies to make change, and that young people were at the center of our work. And I was really interested in how to extend power or recognize power, I should say, in all the ways that it exists. I felt Skillman gave me an opportunity to practice those things.

Matt:

Was there something that drove you to move out to Detroit?

Power:

You know, there was a racial awakening or reckoning happening. I had actually been doing racial equity work for maybe five or six years before 2020 and had a national network of people who knew I was doing this work. So, these jobs just started coming to me, and they were very prominent and high-profile, mostly on the coasts. Meanwhile, I was changing as a human during COVID, and I realized that's not my idea of success anymore. I really want to be very aligned in purpose and rooted in family.

Skillman was just one of the ones that had come up. The thing that really interested me was the youth component. I had been watching this younger generation for some time now, which I later learned was called Gen Z, and how they were approaching social impact in the field. It was super interesting to me. I was wondering, why are there two co-directors instead of one?

Why is there no hierarchy? What do you mean you're not a nonprofit? You're a cooperative? What do you mean by that? You're about racial justice, police reform, education justice, climate change, and more.

There's an intersectionality, a systems analysis, and a rejection of hierarchy, and all these ideas. I was just saying this to my husband the other day. Finally, I was trying to help my kid with her school, and I was on Zoom calls all day, watching these uprisings happening around the world, and it wasn't me out there in the streets I realized. I've been involved in protests in my life. The last thing I thought I was going to do, and I knew I was going to do, was go out before there was a vaccine, bring my child, wear a mask, and march in the streets. And I watched, realizing, like, I'm old. Young people always lead massive change. My street marching time may have passed, but my revolutionary spirit has taken different forms. I organize in the suites these days.

Here's the reality. We need young people and their ambition and risk tolerance. The Civil Rights Movement was led by young people and today's young people are not only leading, but they're also leading differently.

They know something that I don't know, and I have learned things too. We have different positions on the field to play. And I had a personal moment, one that came to many of us where suddenly we were all very aware of our mortality. In COVID or in times like these, or in times when you've got medical issues you are battling, we are brightly aware that we only have a limited time on the planet. I realized with my time here I want to move barriers away from those that are going to really make change in substantial ways that are beyond my imagination and Skillman and Detroit seem like the opportunity, the place, the city, the state, the time that it might make all of this possible.

Matt:

You have mentioned that there were many things going on at Skillman when you first came in, many different initiatives and cause areas that you focused on. But you made a choice to focus the organization in a very specific way. Can you talk a little bit about what drove that decision?

Power:

Well, I had studied the history of Skillman from afar, even as part of coming into an interview. I read all the documents that the staff had written, including a mid-strategy review. And it's interesting because I run foundations, I've worked in foundations, so I know about the code switching that happens between what the staff wants to do and how they explain it to a board.

And I was reading this and thought, "The staff here are up to some interesting things that are just underneath the surface." I understood enough about Detroit to know that Detroiters don't suffer fools. A lot has been done to Detroit, a lot of philanthropy has been done to Detroit, and a lot of policy has been done to Detroit. Detroiters are naturally skeptical, and they have well-earned skepticism.

And so I came with a desire, a posture—not with a plan, but with a posture. That's what I would say. And it was really understanding that I needed to sit with a lot of people and just listen and remain very open to what I would hear. So I had committed before I came to listen for an entire year and to not make it a platitude. I really tried to sit down and listen.. Some of it was online, some of it was in person, which was unusual since we hadn't been in person for a while. My staff, who had felt a little removed from the community, started to come and join me. It became bigger than just welcoming the Chicago CEO to talk to people. It became a reset for all of us at Skillman to get close to our community again after the covid storm and allow ourselves to be changed together.

We had a set of questions: What do I need to understand about Detroit? What do I need to understand about education here? What do I need to understand about philanthropy? Where have we been helpful? Where might we have we been unintentionally harmful? And the final question was, "You as a person, as a human, as a leader in this moment, as a young person navigating all this, as a teacher in the classroom, what do you need? What do you need right now?"

The conversations changed us. We took notes and would respond in seven days with, "Here's what we heard. Is this what you said?" And we started building from there. What did they say they wanted? They wanted transparency. They didn't want this to be the only time that we came out and asked questions. They fundamentally wanted things to change in Detroit. They wanted wholesale system change, and they didn't want to be left out of it. They wanted us to move fast, give differently, be creative, get out of our own way, be less bureaucratic, and to believe in folks and trust people.

And so, when we reached the end of that year, we knew that we had to build deeply on what we've done in the past that has worked so well and in new ways had to change deeply based on what the current moment called for. As we started to build based on it, the second year was a Co-Design Tour where it was like, "Here's what we're doing. Does this make sense?"

This strategy change took a while. Nothing is ever as deeply, authentically co-built as that term implies, because you're still making the decisions and packaging it. But it was a much different process than I have ever been a part of or ever seen. And I'm grateful for it.

Matt:

I know that you did make a choice to be involved in government at all levels. Can you describe that how you currently work with government?

Power:

Well we are involved in policy as it moves at all levels in the public sector and yes, I'll give you an example. After-school is a really good example. That was a body of work where Skillman would fund some after-school programs. What we realized is that through our funding, we were able to help 4,000 young people a year, which is pretty cool and pretty good. But there are 120,000 young people in Detroit. Our dollars were helping only a tiny fraction, and all young people need exposure and access to after school programs in order to really thrive.

So what we did was in partnership with the Ralph C. Wilson Foundation and the CS Mott Foundation. We funded two staff roles at MASP, which is the Michigan After School Partnership in the governor's office. Due to education advocacy around the state, for the first time, three years ago, there was $50 million put in the budget for after-school programs in Michigan. The two staff roles were able to make sure that it was distributed equitably across the state. Another $50 million was put in the budget this past year, and then $75 million.

And so, supporting grassroots and grasstops advocates to push for more support for after school programs helped to get new dollars in the budget for after school. On top of that our help in building capacity in the governor's office helped with implementation of a new massive budget line to make sure those across the state who need it most can have access to it. This takes our impact exponentially higher than were it was when we were funding a few programs here and there, even though I can tell you the programs we were funding were and are phenomenal. But going back to what people told us in the Listening Tour—we need to work on systems and try to make big change. Helping a few here and there is no longer good enough.

That's just an example of how we work. It is not in isolation. We are not only working with grassroots and grasstops and government officials, but we're actually looking at the education ecosystem of change, and we're trying to ignite different circles that need to collaborate for some action.

Matt:

You've got a great corporate background that many people don't know about. But talk to me about corporate partnerships. Are you working with Michigan corporates to get some of your efforts done?

Power:

Yeah, absolutely. When I first came to Skillman, I looked at the board and I was like, this is such an interesting foundation board because there are titans of industry. And it was a thoughtful calculation on how change happens in Michigan, going back to that ecosystem. We have like twelve bubbles in the mapped education ecosystem of how education systems change happens and business is a huge part of it.

In some ways, companies have more impact on policy than Congress. We know that even at a local level, many of our politicians listen to businesses. And if we have an opportunity, which we do, to actually move the education conversation to be something that is co-owned, we do. People are realizing their workforce issues go right back to K-12. We believe that having them in the room, hearing from folks on the ground, hearing from young people, that we have an opportunity to help them help the rest of us.

Matt:

How do you work with nonprofits at Skillman? And what's changed over the past few years?

Power:

I think what's changed is that we talk about all the capital we have to lend in our partnership with nonprofits that are on the front lines. We have our social capital, our moral capital, we have our intellectual capital, we have our reputational capital, and we have our financial capital. Sometimes in foundations, we really lean on the financial and then ask the nonprofit to deliver on all these grand changes that we want.

But at Skillman, we understand that we're part of that education changemaking ecosystem. We aren't the entire ecosystem; we're not in control of the ecosystem and we're certainly not the puppeteer. But funders are one circle in this education changemaking ecosystem. And so we can deploy dollars, but that's a fraction of the tools we can leverage. And even then after wielding everything we've got, it's still up to the collective wisdom and the collective will to make change happen.

Matt:

Can you talk to me about the balance between addressing short-term crises versus long-term systemic change? I see you as a great advocate for balance.

Power:

I think that you can't only do one or the other. You actually have to do both. So we think of it as leaving the light on. I think there was like a Red Roof Inn commercial from back in the day that was like, "we'll leave the light on for ya," That's us at Skillman—we have a strategy to work with grassroots and grasstops to make bigtime education policy change with and for Detroiters—but we will always try to find some kind of way to support outside of the strategy with something, however small.

But to make that change, we had to get really clear about what and who we serve. Who do we serve? We serve Detroit young people. And so what are our values? We are grounded in racial equity and justice, we are youth-driven, accountable to each other, greater than grants and listeners and learners. These are our core values that we have used as a rubric to make decisions.

In order to not be constantly running after emergencies that are relentless, we look at what does it have to do with young people? Is it closely adjacent to education? We have to get to brass tacks. The majority of our budget is for this strategy and for the long term. But we have about a fourth of the budget that's set aside for civic partnerships, which is how we can show up as a good neighbor for adjacent systems that affect young people. Then there's a president's discretionary, which is a rapid response fund.

Matt:

Talk to me about equity and social justice. And how those two concepts play for you at Skillman.

Power:

Equity is an engine, a decision-making engine, an analysis engine that allows you to achieve your mission, to serve, and to create change faster and more efficiently.

It is not a buzzword, and it is not a T-shirt, and it is not a random illegal threat. It is a responsibility and a tool to identify who you want to impact. Let's look at who is most harmed and let's put them in the center, and then let's actually build around them.

Because we know that if we center those who are most harmed by any sort of policy or need, and we make sure that they are okay, and that we change our policies and systems to accommodate them, the echo effect of so many people who are helped is everyone. Everyone benefits from that.

If you are not using an equity lens, which is a balance, a tool of balancing, to make sure that your efforts are impactful and effective, then you're wasting money, you're wasting time, and you're doing all of these efforts that make no sense.

So, in Detroit, a majority Black city, and in public education, especially in Detroit, we are in the high 90% of Black and brown brilliant young people that are in the systems that were built for the 1950s and for different industries. It would be irresponsible to not actually use a racialized analysis and an equitable approach to the work that we do. Period.

You know, the social justice piece is that there's a lot of space for folks in the social impact world. There is the direct service that you need to do every single day because people are dying. We just had two children freeze to death in a van in a casino parking lot overnight because the mother was there with her five children and had been rejected from so many different places where she was seeking shelter. We need a solution for that right now. Children should not be dying in casino parking lots because the mother cannot provide a space for them; we all need to own this failure.

Social justice is the work that we do so that the mother doesn't have to be in that situation in the first place. And also so that the city or these other spaces are bolstered up to not just help in a pinch but to move the needle in terms of nourishment and getting people the resources they need before it ever gets to that.

I think there's a misunderstanding in this world right now, because these terms have been villainized and they're so misunderstood that obviously I feel the need to not just say them but explain them.

Matt:

Can you talk more in detail about how you engage the community, how you bring that out in them while you have a set of opinions that you're trying to get through as well?

Power:

I can talk about the give and take involved in engaging young people authentically. The truth is I I've learned a lot from young people. I've been able to engage with them in incredible ways, and I've also been checked by them and educated about what I can do better. I've learned that when we say "youth-driven," we have to know exactly what we mean. We used to say it often—but now we are much more clear. Skillman, as an organization, while doing really innovative work putting young people in the driver's seat, we are not solely a youth-driven organization. The reality is, we have pockets of opportunities where we open the door and we really do want young people to get in there, to mess it up, to change it around, and do that. This is super innovative and cool and we are learning as we go. And, we also feel we have a responsibility to pull back the curtain on the philanthropic world and explain how it works, because that philanthropic world that I talked about at the beginning with you, which I never knew existed when I was younger, is now something I see and understand. We have a responsibility to make sure young people see it too, that they know this is what's there. I think of that as an answer to your question, about the push and pull within true community engagement work. I show up honestly, with my genuine self, who I am. I know I'm not the expert. Thank God I'm not the smartest person in the world, or else we would all be in big trouble. I know that we need people who are deep Detroiters, who understand this, to find the solutions and lead the way. And with my fallible human ways, I still have other things to offer. We are afforded a unique position inside of a foundation, a perch that is different from what most people have. I think it's important to come correct and to be very clear that you are still a person with all your faults, you want partnership, and it's a give and take and everyone will grow and change.

We all have a responsibility, and we all have a unique voice that's important. I am Black and Jewish, the youngest of six, the child of a teacher and a cop from the southside of Chicago. I think as an artist. A writer. And I'm always going to show up fully myself and not expect to meld into some other thing. I feel like it's easier for me to just show up as an individual and be myself and try to be in a real trusting relationship. I think all of that helps.

Matt:

What advice would you give to a young person not brand new to this environment, but sort of been through a couple of struggles already and starting to move forward? If they are asking "Am I going to commit my life to this or not?" what advice would you have for them?

Power:

I would say, "We need you. Don't give up, because we need you. The world will be improved because of what you've seen, what you've experienced, and how you imagine a different space for the future.

Young people bring an intersectional analysis. They bring in hopefulness. They have less fidelity to party or to institution or to traditional practice. And I think that, you know, we talk about how the frontal lobe hasn't fully formed yet until someone is in their mid-twenties as a bad thing. But actually, there's a benefit to not having your frontal lobe fully formed, and that is that you are a natural risk-taker. This is why every social change movement that changed our country has been led by young people. They are willing to risk it all for a better world. And in this moment of possibility, we need those willing to push for something better, ideally human centered, fair, just and fulfilling for so many different types of people.

And if we do not take that risk right now, then we will not have the change on the other side of this. So please don't give up. We need you.

"It Takes Broad Community Collaboration to Drive Real Impact"
—Nadege Souvenir, Chief Executive Officer, San Antonio Area Foundation

Matt:

Please describe your background in philanthropy, including what led up to where you are and what you're doing now in San Antonio.

Souvenir:

I have been in philanthropy for 10 years now, and I started in philanthropy at the St. Paul and Minnesota Foundation on their grants and programs. I was part of the community impact team, leading the operational back end. Then, I got promoted to vice president of learning and operations, and then as SVP, and ultimately was the chief operating officer of the largest community foundation in Minnesota.

Now I'm the CEO of the San Antonio Area Foundation, leading the oldest community foundation in Texas and one of the largest community foundations in the country.

Matt:

You've taken some creative approaches to volunteer support. Is there anything you'd like to call out in terms of volunteer support that would help your organization be even more successful? Is there anything that you'd like to let folks know that you've funded in the past year or so?

Souvenir:

We certainly have funded and been funded for work related to Catchafire. Having skilled based volunteers working with the nonprofit sector is important because often organizations, particularly at the varying stages of their organizational life cycle, don't have the resources to get the type of talent they need to set up infrastructure.

We use volunteers actively in some of our grantmaking work and some of our scholarship work, which is a way to get the local community engaged in better understanding the role that the Community Foundation can play as a backbone to the nonprofit sector.

Matt:

Can you talk a little bit about how you work with the corporate sector?

Souvenir:

Absolutely. The reality is the Community Foundations and the private sector have shared goals and shared alignment. Corporations are looking for successful markets with thriving economies and a talented and available workforce. There are opportunities for alignment that make sense.

For example, in San Antonio, after the murder of George Floyd, a couple of key corporate partners came together and created the Corporate Partners for Racial Equity. The San Antonio Area Foundation served as the backbone of that work. Getting key resources to nonprofit organizations, startups, and businesses led by black and brown folks and really ensuring financial equity, economic equity and focusing on those things. When I was in Minneapolis and St. Paul, working with corporations on issues was a fairly regular occurrence.

There were downtown revitalization initiatives. It was an interesting intersection where the Community Foundation, I think for the first time in its history, was giving grants to small businesses to help them revitalize the main streets of the key areas that got impacted in both St. Paul and Minneapolis.

Right now there's the GroundBreak Coalition in the Twin Cities that is a combination of public-private partnership around wealth equity primarily for Black residents, and the Community Foundation is a partner.

Matt:

Could you describe what you see as the current state of philanthropy? What trends are shaping the sector right now?

Souvenir:

I think 2020 was a pivotal point for philanthropy. Prior to that point, there was that tension and push and pull with nonprofits, begging philanthropy to do more general operating, more multiyear, more trust-based philanthropy. And there was maybe some resistance or sluggishness to move in that direction. And then 2020 hit, and all of a sudden philanthropy did it in a heartbeat.

What is interesting now is watching some reversion back to sort of specific programmatic dollars, but also some folks staying the course on general operating support and multiyear grantmaking.

The other thing that we're seeing in philanthropy, not just in the foundation sector, but if you think of philanthropy as a larger whole, including corporate philanthropy and even individual philanthropy, is a realignment of priorities.

I think that philanthropy is cyclical. There are periods of time where certain issues are the focus. And so we're seeing a shift away from, or a refocused lens on, where there might have been arts and culture and cultural vibrancy to looking instead at education or health. Even more specifically for corporate philanthropy, looking at what their line of business is and what the literal issue associated with the line of business is in the community.

Matt:

Talk to me a little bit about the shifts that you've seen in donor expectations and engagement.

Souvenir:

I come from a market that had a culture of philanthropy, laid out by corporate leaders challenging their peers. There was the 5% challenge, and it was almost like a contest: who could be the most philanthropic corporate partner. That trickled into individual philanthropy and foundational philanthropy. What we're seeing is a shift in that sort of prominence in that market.

There isn't an expectation that you just do it because you have to. Instead, there's a question of how it's related and aligned to goals or to our bottom line. And that's not a bad thing, but it definitely impacts the sector that was used to saying, "yes, this community understands that giving is what it does."

What I have observed on the donor side is that post-George Floyd, there was a lot of money and resources going to organizations that had not previously received those dollars and hadn't previously gotten any attention. Suddenly in some instances, little, tiny organizations were getting millions of dollars in the span of a couple of days. Then there was a turnaround, like, "What are you going to do with it?" As if they had secret game plans for multimillion-dollar infusions, because nobody was expecting that. There is a little bit of an ROI expectation that is coming from individual donors, as well as foundations and corporations too. But this isn't widgets, right?

This is people; this is social issues. You can't just say, "Thanks, you gave me a million dollars, and here's exactly how many people's lives I've changed." But you can say, "You gave me a million dollars, and now I could actually pay my staff, and now I have a team of 10 people, and now we can actually do more."

I think there's a tension there in understanding the nature of the work, and I think there's a shifting in generational expectations around philanthropy. There's a generation that understands GoFundMe's and campaigns. They understand aligning their philanthropy to the things they care about or the things they can get their hands dirty with and volunteer for, and all of that is great. But the group of folks who operated more as benefactors. . . that's changing.

Matt:

Are there other learnings that we should be taking from the way priorities changes after that George Floyd and the way that it's kind of backtracking right now? What can we learn from that experience?

Souvenir:

One of the things we can learn is that all the stuff we claimed was hard and needed time, we could actually do. Philanthropy likes to talk about itself as a big ship that takes a really long time to turn. Maybe, but there are actually ways to press a button and move a lot faster.

That's one of the learnings I hope philanthropy keeps and recognizes—there is a nimbleness inherent in how we do the work. We don't always have to be moving at that speed, but when the moment calls for it, we can do it.

Matt:

How do you balance the need of short-term crisis response in the hunger perspective, that means we need to feed folks that are hungry today, then how do you balance that against long-term strategic systemic solutions?

Souvenir:

That's a particularly interesting challenge for a community foundation, because we care about a place and it's within our ethos that we're supposed to care about that place into perpetuity.

We can't just open up our coffers and say, "Here is all the money for the food today," because that wouldn't actually support the need to be there 10 years, 20 years, 30 years, 100 years from now.

When I look at the grantmaking here and in other community foundations, it does seem like there are some resources dedicated to immediate short-term needs and some resources dedicated to longer-term sort of planning and solutions. One of the things that we do here is get involved in key initiatives. That's a way that we're driving toward that longer-term success.

We are an anchor partner of something called Future Ready Bexar County, which has an ultimate goal by 2030 of getting 70% of graduating high school students in Bexar County enrolled in degree credentialed or accredited programs. When that work started, it was at 52%. So that's a pretty long-term sort of stretch. Yet some of our partners involved in that work need money right now to buy the supplies to go into the schools to do the work.

I think one of the particular ways a foundation can do that is maybe you have a couple of core large initiatives that are focused on the longer term, and then the grantmaking can be focused on meeting the immediate needs of the nonprofits doing the work.

Matt:

Trust in philanthropy has changed in multiple different ways and maybe in different directions over the past five years. Can you discuss what foundations can do to strengthen trust in philanthropy?

Souvenir:

The fact that we needed the concept of trust-based philanthropy is an interesting concept in itself. But it makes sense because philanthropy, at its origin, started with the concept of charity. Like, "I'm going to willingly give you a little bit. And therefore I feel good about myself and you're a little bit better." The move in the last few years is trying to address the inherent power balance of the fact that one of us has money to give and one of us needs the money. There will always be a power imbalance in that scenario, no matter how good the trust is.

I think about how foundations can be more transparent about their processes and how they give dollars. There were periods probably at almost every foundation where it was like, "well, the only way you get money is if you know someone or do you know the CEO." And now it's more about being more open about processes, clearer about the opportunities, and acknowledging that not all nonprofits are created equal.

I think that openness in dialogue is probably the biggest and most important piece of trust-based philanthropy. I know a lot of people point to the general operating and the multiyear grants, and I agree. All of those things are great, but not every foundation is in a position to do those things. I don't think it's not trust-based philanthropy just because it's not multiyear and or not general operating. It's trust-based philanthropy if it's apparent we're not wasting people's time. We're not asking them to create programs to bend to our need to tell a story. We're letting them do the work.

Matt:

Let's take a shift into organizations not having to shoulder all of the responsibility themselves anymore. Talk a bit about partnerships or collaborations that have helped you the most over your career, either in your previous role or in the role that you're in now.

Souvenir:

Honestly, I think that to solve any of the intractable problems, the ones that are core to who we are, hunger, poverty and jobs, organizations can't shoulder it alone. None of these sectors can do it by themselves; not a single one of them can do it by themselves. And we all have different roles that we play in this ecosystem and different levers that we can pull. What I've observed is that where you can get a public-private partnership collaboration, things can actually happen. It's really hard to get to that agreement though, right?

Where I have seen the most movement is where there could be some agreement. Saying something like, "Hey, collectively, we're going to focus not on a narrow, but rather a well-defined charge." Then independently, we will still do what we do, independently, related to that area and that field.

Matt:

The organizations you're a part of deeply tap into the communities themselves, as opposed to coming from the top down with edicts about how the world should work. Explain a bit about how you engage with the communities that you serve. What does the process look like for you?

Souvenir:

When the process is working as it should, community is informing the process throughout. Let's take our open grant program, for example. We've set up that program, specifically capacity-building grants, because we had information that let us know the community needed or wanted that. Then you get the applications and make decisions about who gets grants and who doesn't. There's information there that the community is giving us, and so we can ask if this grant is actually meeting the need. Or we realize we're denying a bunch of applicants that look very similar. Should we be doing something else for that group?

Next the grants go out and the nonprofits do the work, and there's opportunity in either reporting or follow-up conversations to learn from what outcomes are resulting. In an ideal universe, this is like a slowly revolving wheel that is moving along and adapting as necessary to meet the community's needs. We're not just saying, "Hey, we talked to them five years ago, we set up a grant program, we're done." It's always being in conversation and recognizing that conversation does not necessarily mean we held a community convening last week. We're in conversation all the time. The big question is, what are we doing with that information? Are we just letting it go to the wayside or actually letting it inform the very next step that we take?

Matt:

What advice do you have for those younger leaders looking for guidance? What guidance would you give them about what they should be doing in the near future?

Souvenir:

One of the pieces of guidance is to have patience. And I say that as an impatient person, but the sorts of things that we are trying to change took decades or hundreds of years to get to this moment. There isn't a quick fix and a quick solution. There is sort of intentional, steady, repeated progress and work toward a goal. And, you know, when you are just getting into that space, that can feel really unfulfilling.

It's not as easy as it seemed before I got involved in a foundation. It's not like. "We care about hunger. No one is hungry in our city anymore." I wish it were that easy. You have to find the small wins where you can find them and acknowledge movement through the process along the way.

I think the other piece of advice I have is that entrepreneurism and innovation belong in this space. Sometimes they're talked about like a separate thing for entrepreneurs over there starting businesses hoping to get bought out. Genius needs to be inside of foundations. Genuis needs to be in the next big way that philanthropy can do stuff. It needs to be a part of the entire nonprofit sector. So those folks who are naturally inclined to entrepreneurship and innovation should not shy away from using those skills to move philanthropy forward.

Summary and What's Ahead

In this chapter we heard from the folks on the front lines of the four forces to talk about what they see. From Governor Jim Doyle we heard that we cannot let government off the hook when it comes to their responsibility to build strong communities as well as that each of the four forces have individuals willing and able to help out, including corporations. From Ginny Finn we heard philanthropy and foundations do indeed face a number of challenges currently and historically, but that examples abound of all four forces working together to build stronger communities. From Walter Lanier we heard about the profound lack of coordination between the four forces and also that the nonprofit and foundation sectors desperately need to let the community be an integral part of what they do every day. From Deb Fowler we heard that when foundations understand nonprofits and governments actively partner with nonprofits, the communities we serve get stronger. From Angelique Power we heard that the youth in our communities serve a unique and important part in building strong communities and we have an obligation to empower them to attain success. And from Nadege Souvenir we heard that it takes broad community involvement to drive the significant impact that each of us seeks. Now let's focus on wrapping up the book and understand the call to action!

CHAPTER 9

Start Small but Start Now!

"Young people bring in intersectional analysis. They bring in hopefulness. They have less fidelity to party or to institution or to traditional practice . . . (the young) are natural risk-takers.

And if we do not take that risk right now, then we will not have the change on the other side of this. So please don't give up. We need you."

—Angelique Power, President & CEO,
Skillman Foundation

If you've made it this far, you've read my analysis of the current state of philanthropy, nonprofits, government, and business. You've had the chance to consider the steps I believe can and must be taken to course correct where our society is headed. You've seen some effective foundational actions detailed in the Perseverance Playbook. And I hope you've been buoyed by the many interviews sharing insights and work being done by progressive leaders who are tackling difficult issues in diverse ways across the United States. What remains to be done? I want to convince you to get involved now.

The Curse of Complacency

Younger readers may not know much about the struggles their grandparents, parents, aunts, uncles, and long-time family friends engaged in many years ago. While the decades between the 1950s and 2000s may seem like ancient history, important changes came about that made our country safer, healthier, more equitable, and freer. Civil rights, women's rights, LGBTQ rights, clean air and water, consumer protections, even the creation of small but once-unthinkable practices like smoke-free environments. Perhaps those who fought these battles and those who were born into a more just society began to take for granted these many freedoms and protections. We thought there would be no going back to the bad old days. We got complacent.

The promise of America has always been that tomorrow will be better than today, for everyone. The prospect of a brighter future is what has attracted talented people to our shores since colonial times. For better or worse, the world has seen Americans as the people who are never satisfied with the way things are. People who never stop innovating, discovering, rethinking, rebuilding. A distinctly American culture convinced that the job of each generation is to leave behind a better world for their children and grandchildren.

When did you lose that spirit? Why do so many of us no longer believe progress is possible?

Complacency will be the end of this country. We simply cannot let that happen. I am and always will be an activist and a believer in the power of activism. My hope for this book is that it will encourage you to join me and millions of like-minded people who refuse to go backward. We are unwilling to surrender our belief in the promise of America. That means we can never be satisfied with the status quo. The lack of concrete progress now can't be allowed to make us quit. We have to fulfill our obligation to the future to build the bridges and ladders for those coming up behind us. Across the generational gaps, we must unite to push for a country that is always moving forward for everyone. The American dream has yet to be fulfilled. The mountain of work ahead can seem daunting. Like any big venture, I urge you to start small. Do a few things you are comfortable with, then move on to some that are less comfortable. Think of this as a sort of road map to get going on a path to meaningful change keeping in mind what Speaker of the House Tip O'Neill wisely noted, "All politics is local." Start there. Don't depend on the federal government being there for us all. Start in your communities. And start today.

Thanks, Tom Peters

From my earliest childhood politics was a favorite topic for family discussion. My parents instilled in me the importance of engagement and awareness. But once I was out making my way in the world, I slipped into a "I'm just a cog in the wheel" mentality. At the time I was working in state government and while I had a fancy title of CIO I thought of myself as the lowly IT guy in a vast bureaucracy. Then I read business thought leader Tom Peters's book, *Re-imagine*. It changed my world. I went on to devour everything else Peters wrote but the seminal idea was this—I can drive change from wherever I sit in an organization. I stopped thinking I couldn't possibly make a difference from so far down in the org chart.

Peters's book challenged me to figure out what my role actually was in the hierarchy and what that enabled me to achieve from the inside. The difference between feeling like a cog and feeling like an engine was exhilarating. It powered me and my incredible team at the little old Division of Enterprise Technology to drive changes that were not just better for the government and for the citizenry. We made changes that were amazing, in large part because we believed we could. I carried that ethic with me, to Microsoft, to Salesforce, to Digital Realty, to Socrata, to AkitaBox, and to Catchafire. One small boy raised by a single mom, I took all of her lessons, with a tad bit of passion, and brought change to the world most places I went.

As you read through the interviews in Chapter 8, you encountered a variety of people with different backgrounds and experience who perhaps share a few traits in common. They saw a problem they felt needed to be solved and they believed they should be the one to tackle it. They were not held back by not knowing the answer at the outset. They were willing to put in the time, do the work, enlist the aid of others, and build a movement. None of them could have foreseen the setbacks and successes ahead. But each was willing to keep pushing from wherever they were in an organization or in society. The world is in debt to each of them, as am I.

Choosing Your Fight

We're struggling through an overwhelming time of societal dysfunction, so it is understandable to be paralyzed by the "flood the zone" tactics of those trying to protect or preserve their own privilege. It is futile for us as individuals to wage a battle on multiple fronts. Instead I want you to ask yourself, "What issue matters most to me?" Once you can land on a single target, start with what you know about this situation. Who is at risk? Who are the aggressors? What societal forces are engaged? Which are on the sidelines?

If you start with what you know, you can begin to look for possible openings for action. Start small. Keep getting more information. Take some initial steps with something that is right in front of you, something that is not filled with conflict and difficulty. Maybe that means joining an existing group that is local, regional, or even national. Successfully completing some small steps of engagement helps build confidence and momentum. Arm yourself with the understanding that affecting change is going to get more difficult. But with persistence and small wins to aid you, when the hard things come you've earned the confidence to do what you need to do.

One practice that compels me in this space is the notion of deliberately creating "common ground." Right now when so much of what we thought was settled is being overturned daily, the world seems willing to reconfigure what we believed was true. Traditional political parties are willing to throw everything up in the air and figure out something substantially different. This is the time when we are most open to sitting down and talking to each other. I'm not saying this is easy, but it is within our reach. Break bread with people who disagree with each other. Be choosy about the food because no one argues when the food is good—where I come from in Milwaukee it's a fish fry that unites us. Find the neutral ground, provide regionally relevant food, and have real, consciously focused conversations. Ideally the folks around the table should come from all the four forces of nonprofits, philanthropy, government, and business. See where the conversation takes you. Work on something lower in conflict, easier to accomplish, where you have the most probability of success. It may be the first step in building a powerful coalition.

The Perseverance Playbook detailed in Chapter 7 can be a useful guide. It can help you form a new group or aid an existing group in expanding their outreach and increasing their chances for scoring some victories. Whether you are getting that first meeting off the ground for a new entity or bringing fresh energy and strategies to an existing group, you are making progress. Take at least one step outside your comfort zone. It's impossible to predict the outcome but I can state with certainty that if you don't dive in, nothing will happen as you hoped.

I also cannot stress enough the importance of preparing mentally and physically for the cadence of change. More often than not it can feel like one step forward and two steps back. The winners are the ones who commit to the long game, like the Cypherpunks.

Quit Complaining, Start Coding

Although it is nearly impossible to imagine a world before social media, in the 1980s and 1990s forming an electronic mailing list was still something of a novelty as was the practice of cryptography or privacy-enhancing technology. The "Cypherpunks" were a loose amalgamation of tech-savvy folks who shared a concern for what they perceived to be an ever-growing capability for covert surveillance by government or corporate players. Over time members tired of the endless repetition of fears and angry outbursts. This decentralized, defiantly libertarian group formed a leaderless entity, a "virtual" community that was determined to stop whining and to fight back using the tools they had, namely their ability to write code. "Cypherpunks write code" was their mantra. Cypherpunks became a powerful movement dedicated to taking action. Their initial work resulted in an effective encryption program that was modestly dubbed "Pretty Good Privacy" (PGP). This was activism at its most direct. Cypherpunks didn't lobby for change. They created it.

Before dismissing this as old news, it's worth noting that the Cypherpunk mindset and approach laid the foundation for technologies that have shaped contemporary communication through messaging, privacy practices for web browsers, and global finance. There's a direct line from their "shut up and code" approach to the formation of bitcoin. And the newest looming tech threat and promise is already here, AI. If you don't believe the world is about to change just use any of the AI versions easily available and suddenly ubiquitous. You'll quickly realize how fundamentally everything is going to change. If we don't build strong communities now our neighborhoods, towns, and cities will be devastated when there are no jobs and no compensation to be had because technologies controlled by a few have taken them over. And as I have said throughout this book, AI can be leveraged. If it is for good or not is entirely up to you.

It's Your Time

Even a casual glance at the headlines spotlights unprecedented upheavals in what many of us had come to believe was the "natural order of things," with changes here at home rippling out into global repercussions. The US government is withdrawing from major investment in R&D, global humanitarian aid, science and technology, education, and a social safety net. Corporations are facing unstable trade policies, economic challenges to globalization and expansion, consolidation and monopolies, high barriers to entry in key industries, labor shortages, and extreme emphasis placed on stock valuation and quarterly returns. Philanthropy, despite the billions it controls, is under-resourced to fill all the gaps created by government and corporate withdrawals and reversals. Meanwhile a huge transfer of wealth as boomers retire will make billions more available for investment in social change. Nonprofits sit at the bottom of the food chain, wholly dependent on government, corporate, and philanthropic dollars to fund the essential work they provide as boots on the ground. The nonprofit sector is likely to experience massive rates of failure resulting in condemning more millions of underserved people to extreme risk for health and safety.

That's a lot of doom and gloom but it is also the reason I believe now is the time to get active. Older folks can and will be supportive, but this is not their fight. They are not the ones to lead a push forward. As Angelique Power said at the start of this chapter, we need younger people to take on the challenge. Professionals in the early or mid-stages of their careers already have a lot to manage with work and family but they cannot disengage and think someone else will take care of fixing things. I worry that too many, whether they are in government, business, or philanthropy, have checked out. They have not heard Tom Peters's message as I did, that we are all capable of bringing about substantive change from where we sit today.

It's hard and it is asking a lot, but we all need you to take heart. Find the energy to work for the world you know we can achieve. Together we can rebuild our broken systems.

Notes

Chapter 1

1. Gallup, Inc. (2007b, October 12). *Satisfaction with the United States*. Gallup.com. https://news.gallup.com/poll/1669/general-mood-country.aspx.
2. Team, C. (2024, August 2). *Kondratieff wave*. Corporate Finance Institute. https://corporatefinanceinstitute.com/resources/economics/kondratieff-wave/.
3. Bell, P., & Bell, P. (2025, August 12). *Public Trust in Government: 1958–2024*. Pew Research Center. https://www.pewresearch.org/politics/2024/06/24/public-trust-in-government-1958-2024/.
4. Aguiar, M. (2022, May 20). *What AI reveals about trust in the world's largest companies*. BCG. https://www.bcg.com/publications/2022/trust-index-analyzing-companies-trustworthiness.
5. In a 1982 address to CPAC (Conservative Political Action Conference), Reagan claimed that "Higher productivity, a larger gross national product, a healthy Dow Jones average—they are our goals and are worthy ones."
6. Lewis, S. (2024, January 11). *Top 4 priorities nonprofits must tackle in 2024*. OneCause. https://www.onecause.com/blog/top-4-priorities-nonprofits-must-tackle-in-2024/.
7. *Interactive: How key groups of Americans voted in 2024*. (2024, November 7). PBS News. https://www.pbs.org/newshour/politics/interactive-how-key-groups-of-americans-voted-in-2024-according-to-ap-votecast.
8. Brown, M., Figueroa, F., Fingerhut, H., & Sanders, L. (2024, November 10). *Election 2024: How and why young Black and Latino men chose Trump | AP News*. AP News. https://apnews.com/article/young-black-latino-men-trump-economy-jobs-9184ca85b1651f06fd555ab2df7982b5.

9. Lindsay, J. M. (2024, December 18). *The 2024 election by the numbers*. Council on Foreign Relations. https://www.cfr.org/article/2024-election-numbers.

Chapter 2

1. Hartmann, M. E. (2020, July 27). *How much money is in nonprofit endowments in America?* Philanthropy Daily. https://philanthropydaily.com/how-much-money-is-in-nonprofit-endowments-in-america/.

2. Peterson-Withorn, C. (2024, April 2). *Forbes' 38th Annual World's Billionaires List: Facts and figures 2024*. Forbes. https://www.forbes.com/sites/chasewithorn/2024/04/02/forbes-38th-annual-worlds-billionaires-list-facts-and-figures-2024/.

3. Statista. (2024, August 7). *U.S. billionaires 1990-2023*. https://www.statista.com/statistics/220093/number-of-billionaires-in-the-united-states/.

4. Napoletano, E. (2023, October 23). *Here's how many billionaires and millionaires live in the U.S.* Forbes Advisor. https://www.forbes.com/advisor/retirement/how-many-billionaires-and-millionaires-live-in-the-u-s/.

5. Peterson-Withorn, C. (2024b, October 1). *The 2024 Forbes 400 list of wealthiest Americans: facts and figures*. Forbes. https://www.forbes.com/sites/chasewithorn/2024/10/01/the-2024-forbes-400-list-of-wealthiest-americans-facts-and-figures/.

6. Meeks, M., & Meeks, M. (2024, June 25). *Giving USA: U.S. charitable giving totaled $557.16 billion in 2023 | Giving USA*. Giving USA | a Public Service Initiative of the Giving Institute. https://givingusa.org/giving-usa-u-s-charitable-giving-totaled-557-16-billion-in-2023/. The most recent data available as of this writing.

7. *Giving USA*'s website states that its findings are based on "time-tested adherence to using the most rigorous methodologies available for estimating total charitable giving in the U.S. each year."

8. Meeks, M., & Meeks, M. (2024b, June 25). *Giving USA: U.S. charitable giving totaled $557.16 billion in 2023 | Giving USA*. Giving USA | a Public Service Initiative of the Giving Institute. https://givingusa.org/giving-usa-u-s-charitable-giving-totaled-557-16-billion-in-2023/.

9. Lu, M. (2024, February 19). *Visualizing wealth distribution in America (1990-2023)*. Visual Capitalist. https://www.visualcapi talist.com/wealth-distribution-in-america/#google_vignette.
10. *"Wealth," North American Review, June* 1889.
11. Ford Foundation. (2024, April 24). *Our origins - Ford Foundation*. https://www.fordfoundation.org/about/about-the-ford-founda tion/our-origins/.
12. Ibid.
13. $56.7 billion, the extent of Warren Buffett's philanthropic giving to date, for example.
14. Golberg, E. (2024, Dec 7). *What if charity shouldn't be optimized?* New York Times. https://www.nytimes.com/2024/12/07/business/ charity-holiday-giving-optimized.html.
15. Impact Genome, https://www.impactgenome.com/.
16. Internal Revenue Code Section 4942.
17. Heskett, C., & Heskett, C. (2025, March 6). *State of Nonprofits 2024: What funders need to know*. The Center for Effective Philanthropy. https://cep.org/report-backpacks/state-of-non profits-2024-what-funders-need-to-know/?finding=1&slide=3# finding1/slide3.
18. Admin, C. (2024b, February 24). *Greater Milwaukee Foundation exceeds $700 million fundraising goal*. Milwaukee Courier Weekly Newspaper. https://milwaukeecourieronline.com/index .php/2024/02/24/greater-milwaukee-foundation-exceeds-700- million-fundraising-goal/.
19. *"Charitable Giving Statistics"*. NPTrust. 2015-02-17.
20. *Can we utilize endowment to collateralize line of credit?* (n.d.). Nonprofit Issues. https://www.nonprofitissues.com/to-the-point/ can-we-utilize-endowment-collateralize-line-credit.
21. *What every nonprofit should know about UPMIFA Part 1 | Truist*. (n.d.). Truist. https://www.truist.com/resources/wealth/founda tions-endowments/article/what-every-nonprofit-should-know- about-upmifa-part-1.
22. MIPHI | News & Media. (n.d.). https://www.miphi.net/pages/ media_single.html?id=sahrdaya.

Chapter 3

1. Im, C., Grundhoefer, S., Arrillaga, E. S., Buteau, E., Grundhoefer, S., Im, C., Yang, E., Buchanan, P., Bolduc, K., Nicolette, G. C., Babiker, R., & Martin, S. (2024). *State of Nonprofits 2024: What funders need to know*. Center for Effective Philanthropy. https://cep.org/report-backpacks/state-of-nonprofits-2024-what-funders-need-to-know/?section=intro.

2. Ibid.

3. Pipher, M. (2023, December 11). *Finding light in winter*. The New York Times.

4. *Pennsylvania Abolition Society*. (n.d.). https://www.paabolition.org/.

5. Curry, J.L.M. (1898). *A brief sketch of George Peabody and a history of the Peabody Education Fund through thirty years*. Peabody Education Fund.

6. John Thelin, education historian, coined the term.

7. A History of the Tax-Exempt Sector: An SOI Perspective. (2008). In *Statistics of Income Bulletin*. https://www.irs.gov/pub/irs-soi/tehistory.pdf.

8. Writer, S. (2013, October 4). *When government shuts down, the nonprofit community pays*. National Council of Nonprofits. https://www.councilofnonprofits.org/opinions/when-govern ment-shuts-down-nonprofit-community-pays.

9. Haider, D. (2017, February 22). *Nonprofit Mergers: New study sees strategy and success*. Non Profit News | Nonprofit Quarterly. https://nonprofitquarterly.org/nonprofit-mergers-look-contexts-indicators-success.

10. Statista. (2024a, July 5). *U.S. number of nonprofit organizations 1998-2023*. https://www.statista.com/statistics/189245/number-of-non-profit-organizations-in-the-united-states-since-1998/.

11. Ibid.

12. Writer, S. (2025). *Economic impact of nonprofits*. National Council of Nonprofits. https://www.councilofnonprofits.org/about-americas-nonprofits/economic-impact-nonprofits.

13. Ibid.

14. Ariella, S. (2023, May 12). *26 Incredible Nonprofit Statistics [2023]: How many nonprofits are in the U.S.?* Zippia. https://www.zippia.com/advice/nonprofit-statistics/.

15. Meeks, M., & Meeks, M. (2024c, June 25). *Giving USA: U.S. charitable giving totaled $557.16 billion in 2023 | Giving USA*. Giving USA | a Public Service Initiative of the Giving Institute. https:// givingusa.org/giving-usa-u-s-charitable-giving-totaled-557-16- billion-in-2023/.

16. US Census Bureau. (2023, June 13). *At height of pandemic, more than half of people age 16 and over helped neighbors, 23% formally volunteered*. Census.gov. https://www.census.gov/library/stories/ 2023/01/volunteering-and-civic-life-in-america.html.

Chapter 4

1. Partnership for Public Service. (2024, July 24). *Public Trust in Government2024*.https://ourpublicservice.org/publications/state- of-trust-in-government-2024/.

2. Nadeem, R., & Nadeem, R. (2025, April 24). *Americans' Views of Government: Decades of distrust, enduring support for its role*. Pew Research Center. https://www.pewresearch.org/politics/ 2022/06/06/americans-views-of-government-decades-of-distrust- enduring-support-for-its-role/.

3. Conway, N.O.E.M. (2022, November 15). *From Anti-government to anti-science:Why conservatives have turned against science*. American Academy of Arts & Sciences. https://www.amacad.org/ publication/daedalus/anti-government-anti-science-why-con servatives-have-turned-against-science.

4. From a partisan perspective, those who identify as Republicans indicate the greatest level of federal distrust. Jones, J. M. (2023, October 13). *Americans trust local government most, Congress least*. Gallup.com. https://news.gallup.com/poll/512651/ameri cans-trust-local-government-congress-least.aspx.

5. Reid, J.C., Brown, S.J., & Dmello, J. (2023). COVID-19, diffuse anxiety, and Public (Mis)Trust in Government: Empirical insights and implications for crime and justice. *Criminal Justice Review* 49 (2): 117–134. https://doi.org/10.1177/07340168231190673.

6. Hegland, A., Zhang, A.L., Zichettella, B., & Pasek, J. (2022). A partisan pandemic: How COVID-19 was primed for polarization. *The Annals of the American Academy of Political and Social Science* 700 (1): 55–72. https://doi.org/10.1177/0002716222 1083686.

7. Reid, J.C., Brown, S.J., & Dmello, J. (2023b). COVID-19, diffuse anxiety, and Public (Mis)Trust in Government: Empirical insights and implications for crime and justice. *Criminal Justice Review* 49 (2): 117–134. https://doi.org/10.1177/07340168231190673.

8. UNU-WIDER. (2022, June 3). *Keynote address by Sir Tim Besley, "Trust as State Capacity"* [Video]. YouTube. https://www.youtube.com/watch?v=X8mWI-ilHWI.

9. Cohen, R. (2021, June 10). *Breaking down public trust.* Ford School News. https://fordschool.umich.edu/news/2021/rebuilding-trust-in-government-democracy.

10. Dominic Cummings, a senior aide to the British prime minister

11. Fancourt, D. (2020, August 15). The Cummins effect: politics, trust, and behaviours during the COVID-19 pandemic. *The Lancet* https://www.sciencedirect.com/science/article/pii/S0140673620316901.

12. STICERD | Publications | Books. (n.d.). STICERD | Publications | Books. https://sticerd.lse.ac.uk/_new/publications/books/pillars-of-prosperity/.

13. Cummings, R. et al. (2009). Tax morale affects tax compliance: Evidence from surveys and an artefactual field experiment. *Journal of Economic Behavior & Organization* 70 (3): 447–457. http://doi.org/10.1016/j.jebo.2008.02.010.

14. FAQs. (n.d.). https://www.federalreserve.gov/faqs.htm.

15. USAFacts. (2024, December 19). *How many people work for the federal government?* USAFacts. https://usafacts.org/articles/how-many-people-work-for-the-federal-government/.

16. Funkhouser, M. (2021, April 20). *Problems only government can solve.* Governing. https://www.governing.com/gov-institute/on-leadership/gov-problems-only-government-can-solve.html.

17. Fitzgerald, M. F. (2024, June 5). *Some problems, only government can solve.* Harvard Public Health Magazine. https://harvardpublichealth.org/policy-practice/some-problems-only-government-can-solve/.

18. O'Reilly, T. (2011). Government as a Platform. *Innovations: Technology, Governance, Globalization* 6 (1): 13–40. https://direct.mit.edu/itgg/article/6/1/13/9649/Government-as-a-Platform.

19. *Governor Moore signs three executive orders to increase economic development and modernize state government - Press releases - News - Office of Governor Wes Moore*. (n.d.). https://governor.maryland.gov/news/press/pages/governor.moore-signs-three-executive-orders-to-increase-economic-development-and-modernize-state-government.aspx.

20. *Open government*. (n.d.). Data.gov. https://data.gov/open-gov/

21. McCrystal, L. (2019, August 21). *Philly soda tax: Here's how much money it has raised, and how it's been spent*. Inquirer.com. https://www.inquirer.com/news/philly-soda-tax-revenue-spending-20190821.html.

22. *Impact genome*. (n.d.). https://www.impactgenome.com/internal-posts/catchafire-and-impact-genome-join-forces-to-strengthen-social-outcomes-and-philanthropic-impact.

23. *Mission & Values | Third sector Capital Partners*. (2025, March 24). Third Sector Capital Partners. https://www.thirdsectorcap.org/mission/.

24. Peters, B. J. K. S. (n.d.). *How Outcomes-Based Funding Models can Improve the Effectiveness of state and local Governments | What matters: investing in results to build strong, vibrant communities*. https://investinresults.org/chapter/how-outcomes-based-funding-models-can-improve-effectiveness-state-and-local-governments.html.

25. Light, P. C. (2014). *A Cascade of failures: Why government fails, and how to stop it* (By Brookings & New York University). https://wagner.nyu.edu/files/faculty/publications/Light_Cascade_of_Failures_Why_Govt_Fails.pdf.

26. K&L Gates. (n.d.). *Rollbacks and Repeals: How a new administration effectuates policy changes*. https://www.klgates.com/Rollbacks-and-Repeals-How-a-New-Administration-Effectuates-Policy-Changes-12-17-2024.

27. Light, P. C. (2014b). *A Cascade of failures: Why government fails, and how to stop it* (By Brookings & New York University). https://wagner.nyu.edu/files/faculty/publications/Light_Cascade_of_Failures_Why_Govt_Fails.pdf.

Chapter 5

1. Statista. (2025, May 28). *Countries with the largest gross domestic product (GDP) 2025*. https://www.statista.com/statistics/268173/countries-with-the-largest-gross-domestic-product-gdp/.

2. Terrell, E. (2019, January 17). *When a quote is not (exactly) a quote: The Business of America is Business Edition | Inside Adams*. The Library of Congress. https://blogs.loc.gov/inside_adams/2019/01/when-a-quote-is-not-exactly-a-quote-the-business-of-america-is-business-edition/.

3. Denning, S. (2013, June 26). *The origin of "The World's Dumbest Idea": Milton Friedman*. Forbes. https://www.forbes.com/sites/stevedenning/2013/06/26/the-origin-of-the-worlds-dumbest-idea-milton-friedman/.

4. Schwab, K. (2019, December 2). *Davos Manifesto 2020: The Universal Purpose of a Company in the Fourth Industrial Revolution*. World Economic Forum. https://www.weforum.org/stories/2019/12/davos-manifesto-2020-the-universal-purpose-of-a-company-in-the-fourth-industrial-revolution/.

5. *Creating Shared Value - Institute for Strategy and Competitiveness - Harvard Business School*. (n.d.). https://www.isc.hbs.edu/creating-shared-value/Pages/default.aspx.

6. Furness, V. (2025, January 27). *Sustainable funds market inflows halve as ESG falls out of favour*. Reuters. https://www.reuters.com/sustainability/sustainable-finance-reporting/sustainable-funds-market-inflows-halve-esg-falls-out-favour-2025-01-27/.

7. DesJardine, M., & Shi, W. (2022, August 29). *Managing shareholders in the age of stakeholder capitalism*. Harvard Business Review. https://hbr.org/2022/08/managing-shareholders-in-the-age-of-stakeholder-capitalism.

8. Greenhouse, S. (2024, July 8). The resurgence of unions: How strong & how lasting. *SHRM*. https://www.shrm.org/executive-network/insights/people-strategy/resurgence-unions-how-strong-lasting-greehouse-summer-2024.

9. The Harvard Law School Forum on Corporate Governance. (2022, December 9). *PBCs and the pursuit of corporate good*. https://corpgov.law.harvard.edu/2022/12/09/pbcs-and-the-pursuit-of-corporate-good/.

10. Writer, S. (2020, March 16). *2021 Edelman Trust Brometer.* Edelman. https://www.edelman.com/trust/2021-trust-barometer.

11. Komar, B. and Felter, E. (2023, April 26). *Moving from corporate responsibility to impact.* World Economic Forum. https://www .weforum.org/stories/2023/04/moving-from-corporate-responsi bility-to-impact/.

12. Wang, S., & Review, C. L. (2024, April 3). *Corporate racial respon- sibility.* Columbia Law Review. https://columbialawreview.org/ content/corporate-racial-responsibility/.

13. Murray, C. (2025, April 11). *IBM reportedly walks back diversity policies, citing 'Inherent tensions': Here are all the companies rolling back DEI programs.* Forbes. https://www.forbes.com/ sites/conormurray/2025/04/11/ibm-reportedly-walks-back- diversity-policies-citing-inherent-tensions-here-are-all-the-com panies-rolling-back-dei-programs/.

14. Industrialization and Dominant-Minority relations. (n.d.). In *Industrialization and Dominant-Minority Relations* (pp. 76–77). https://uk.sagepub.com/sites/default/files/upm-binaries/13174_ Chapter4.pdf.

15. *Organized labor's complicated history with civil rights - Harvard Law School.* (2025, February 12). Harvard Law School. https:// hls.harvard.edu/today/organized-labors-complicated-history- with-civil-rights/.

16. Schmidt, C. W. (2015, March 2). *The law and economics of the civil rights revolution - Legal History.* Legal History. https://legal hist.jotwell.com/the-law-and-economics-of-the-civil-rights- revolution/.

17. MasterWord. (2023, April 10). *Multicultural consumers - White paper: Banking on diversity - MasterWord.* MasterWord. https:// www.masterword.com/white-paper/banking-on-diversity/.

18. Del Pilar, W., & Del Pilar, W. (2024, September 10). *A brief history of affirmative action and the assault on Race-Conscious admis sions.* EdTrust. https://edtrust.org/blog/a-brief-history-of-affirma tive-action-and-the-assault-on-race-conscious-admissions/.

19. *The diversity bonus.* (n.d.). Google Books. https://books.google. com/books/about/The_Diversity_Bonus.html?id=oz9x DwAAQBAJ.

20. Hunt, V. (2023, December 5). *Diversity matters even more: The case for holistic impact*. McKinsey & Co. https://www.mckinsey.com/featured-insights/diversity-and-inclusion/diversity-matters-even-more-the-case-for-holistic-impact.

21. Wakabayashi, D. (2017, August 7). *Google fires engineer who wrote memo questioning women in tech*. The New York Times. https://www.nytimes.com/2017/08/07/business/google-women-engineer-fired-memo.html.

22. Vieira, H., & Vieira, H. (2019, April 2). *Bias and belief in meritocracy in AI and engineering - LSE Business Review*. LSE Business Review - Social Sciences for Business, Markets, and Enterprises. https://blogs.lse.ac.uk/businessreview/2019/04/03/bias-and-belief-in-meritocracy-in-ai-and-engineering/.

23. Bryant, J. (2024, September 20). *DEI isn't working. Inclusive Economics might*. Time. https://time.com/7022544/inclusive-economics-dei-impact-business/.

24. Zumbansen, P. (2023). The corporation in an age of divisiveness. *U. of Pennsylvania Journal of Business Law*. https://scholarship.law.upenn.edu/cgi/viewcontent.cgi?article=1702&context=jbl.

25. Schmitt, J., & Schmitt, J. (2024, November 20). *Ranking: Fortune's most powerful business leaders*. Poets&Quants for Undergrads. https://poetsandquantsforundergrads.com/rankings/ranking-fortunes-most-powerful-business-leaders/.

26. Neufeld, D. (2024, November 27). *Ranked: The world's 15 most powerful business leaders*. Visual Capitalist. https://www.visualcapitalist.com/ranked-the-worlds-15-most-powerful-business-leaders/.

27. *Enron: The Smartest Guys in the Room (2005) | Watch free documentaries online*. (2005). [Video]. WatchDocumentaries.com. https://watchdocumentaries.com/enron-the-smartest-guys-in-the-room/.

28. Bondarenko, & Peter. (2025, August 19). *Enron scandal | Summary, Explained, History, & Facts*. Encyclopedia Britannica. https://www.britannica.com/event/Enron-scandal.

29. Thomas, B. D. (2022, November 19). *Theranos scandal: Who is Elizabeth Holmes and why was she on trial?* https://www.bbc.com/news/business-58336998.

30. PBS News Weekend. (2022, December 18). *The effects of FTX's collapse on the cryptocurrency industry.* PBS News. https://www.pbs.org/newshour/show/the-effects-of-ftxs-collapse-on-the-cryptocurrency-industry.

31. Reader, T.W., & Gillespie, A. (2024). Target pressure and corporate scandals: a natural language processing investigation of how organizational culture underlies institutional failures. *European Journal of Work and Organizational Psychology* 1–13. https://doi.org/10.1080/1359432x.2024.2398181.

32. Nadeem, R., & Nadeem, R. (2025b, May 6). *How Americans View Future Harms From Climate Change in Their Community and Around the U.S.* Pew Research Center https://www.pewresearch.org/science/2023/10/25/how-americans-view-future-harms-from-climate-change-in-their-community-and-around-the-u-s/.

33. *C&F Porter Novelli.* (n.d.). https://www.candf.com.ng/.

34. Writer, S. (2022, January 18). *2022 Edelman Trust Barometer.* Edelman. https://www.edelman.com/news-awards/2022-edelman-trust-barometer-reveals-even-greater-expectations-business-lead-government-trust.

Chapter 6

1. Popik, B. (2009, June 13). *"All politics is local"* https://barrypopik.com/blog/all_politics_is_local.

2. Goldberg, E., Krolik, A., & Boyce, L. (2025, July 15). *How companies like J&J, Live Nation and Uber are retreating from DEI.* The New York Times. https://www.nytimes.com/interactive/2025/03/13/business/corporate-america-dei-policy-shifts.html.

3. https://www.impactgenome.com/.

Chapter 7

1. Socialtrendspot. (2025). *Nonprofit lifecycle.* https://socialimpactarchitects.com/wp-content/uploads/2025/01/2025-Nonprofit-Lifecycle.pdf.

2. Smith, S., & Smith, S. (2025, January 15). *Nonprofit Lifecycle | Organizational Growth | Nonprofit Growing Pains.* Social Impact Architects. https://socialimpactarchitects.com/nonprofit-lifecycle/.

3. Cnc, T. S. E. C. C. C. (2019, September 7). *Nonprofits fail – Here's seven reasons why – Tracy Ebarb*. NANOE | Charity's Official Website. https://nanoe.org/nonprofits-fail/.

4. Writer, S. (2025, June 23). *SuRVeY: US Nonprofits at critical point as funding for community needs falters*. NonProfit PRO. https://www.nonprofitpro.com/article/survey-us-nonprofits-at-critical-point-as-funding-for-community-needs-falters/.

5. Commerce Institute. (2025, March 27). *What percentage of businesses fail each year? (2025 data)*. https://www.commerceinstitute.com/business-failure-rate/.

6. Murphy, J. and Meyers, C.V. (2008). Rebuilding organizational capacity in turnaround schools. *Educational Management Administration & Leadership* 37 (1): 9–27. https://doi.org/10.1177/1741143208098162.

7. Hasenfeld, Y., & Garrow, E.E. (2012). Nonprofit Human-Service organizations, social rights, and advocacy in a neoliberal welfare state. *Social Service Review* 86 (2): 295–322. https://doi.org/10.1086/666391.

8. Benjamin, L.M. (2012). Nonprofit organizations and outcome measurement: from tracking program activities to focusing on frontline work. *American Journal of Evaluation* 33 (3): 431–447. https://doi.org/10.1177/1098214012440496.

9. Wellens, L., & Jegers, M. (2013). Effective governance in nonprofit organizations: A literature based multiple stakeholder approach. *European Management Journal* 32 (2): 223–243. https://doi.org/10.1016/j.emj.2013.01.007.

10. Lynch-Cerullo, K., & Cooney, K. (2011). Moving from outputs to outcomes: a review of the evolution of performance measurement in the human service nonprofit sector. *Administration in Social Work* 35 (4): 364–388. https://doi.org/10.1080/03643107.2011.599305.

11. Heinrich, C.J. (2002). Outcomes–Based Performance management in the public sector: Implications for government accountability and effectiveness. *Public Administration Review* 62 (6): 712–725. https://doi.org/10.1111/1540-6210.00253.

Acknowledgments

I write this book, completely inspired by and in awe of the women in my life who have made me who I am. I see this book as a passing of the torch to creative thinkers including my incredible wife, Kathleen, who brings her own revolution to every cause she engages; my two conquering daughters, Madison and Emma; their significant others, Becky and Lucille; every woman I have worked for and with (including those great women who helped write this book), and most inspirationally, my mom. These women and many others showed me the struggles, the traps, the rollercoasters, the violence, the bias, the lack of equity, the exhaustion that comes with being an American woman today. It is time for the face of change to be one showing the strength developed through struggle, not the unfounded confidence that comes from entitlement. Thank you for opening my eyes and for stepping up when the world needs you most.

About the Author

Matt Miszewski has lived within each of the four forces highlighted in his book *Rebuilding Broken Systems*. His experience has shown him the bright parts, dark holes, and opportunities to shine in each of these types of organizations and has informed his advocacy for young participants in these organizations to lead the way to stronger communities.

Born into and raised by a family of labor activists in Milwaukee, Wisconsin, social justice and the empowerment of disenfranchised communities has been core to Matt's life both personally and professionally. A trained civil rights attorney, Matt continued his career in government, first working for Congressman Jerry Kleczka, a member of the powerful Ways and Means Committee, and going on to work for Wisconsin Governor Jim Doyle to strengthen the broken infrastructure of local communities, and has since married his commitment to improving societal inequities with deploying technology solutions for social good at firms including Microsoft, Salesforce, and Socrata.

Matt brings in years of expertise building revolutionary, disruptive technological transformation programs and global GTM strategies that transformed the status quo and has built incredible teams and leaders who have achieved unbelievable goals together. Matt's previous experience includes building out and leading the Public Sector businesses for both Microsoft and Salesforce, building the global revenue organization for Digital Realty Trust (bringing them from $8B in enterprise value to $42B by the time he left nearly four years later), leading the global revenue function at Socrata as Chief Revenue Officer, where he helped governments use data more strategically in the design of their programs, mission, and open government initiatives, and leading AkitaBox, a facilities management SaaS company as CEO. AkitaBox revolutionizes the work and lives of facilities managers and workers around the country.

As CEO of Catchafire, Matt was able to bring his nonprofit experience, technology experience, corporate expertise, and mastery of the public sector together with the power of companies that care about impact and the global foundations that regularly build strong communities. This experience made clear the connection between governments, corporations, nonprofits, and foundations in all of their efforts to make local communities stronger.

Index